20 MINUTE EXERCISES FOR GUITAR

Joseph Federico

Copyright © 2018 Joseph Federico
All rights reserved.
Layout & Design: Carol Milazzo
ISBN-10:0692152512
ISBN-13:9780692152515

I have written this book for the purpose of helping guitarists reach their technical potential on their instrument.

Each section covers a different aspect of guitar playing. The exercises include a cross section of different techniques for both hands.

Taking the sections in the order that they are presented will bring the best results.

The most experienced players can eventually build the exercises up to where they can be played in approximately twenty minutes.

Less experienced players will benefit from mastering each technique in a tempo and time frame that they can control.

The material presented is solely for the purpose of eventual guitar mastery, which the player can apply to any genre of music.

Joseph Federico

CONTENTS

Introduction

1. Tremolo — Pg 1
2. Finger Exercise — Pg 5
3. Shift Exercise — Pg 9
4. Backpicking — Pg 13
5. Alternate Picking — Pg 17
6. Cross Picking — Pg 21
7. Arpeggio — Pg 27
8. Barre Exercises — Pg 31
9. Stretch Exercises — Pg 37
10. Double Stops — Pg 45
11. Double Stop Scales — Pg 55
12. Chord Scales — Pg 63
13. For Beginners — Pg 67

> It is suggested that players read
> through Chapter 13 before
> starting this book.
> The suggestions there will
> expedite the learning processes
> in each of the 12 sections.

1. TREMOLO

The premier exercise for the RIGHT HAND to develop accurate and uniform pick strokes.
This excercise will also develop a comfortable 4 fret stretch in the LEFT HAND.

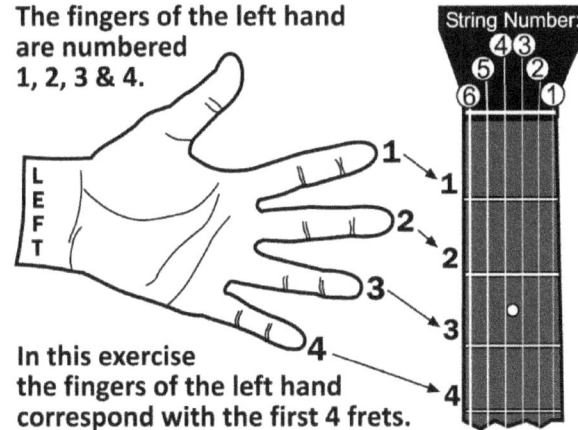

The fingers of the left hand are numbered 1, 2, 3 & 4.

In this exercise the fingers of the left hand correspond with the first 4 frets.

In the Tremolo Excercise the notes of the first 4 frets are repeated 8 times each, while the player concentrates on even and accurate down and up picking.

Beginners should pick with all downstrokes until comfortable.

Play this note 8 times — Use even down & up strokes of the pick

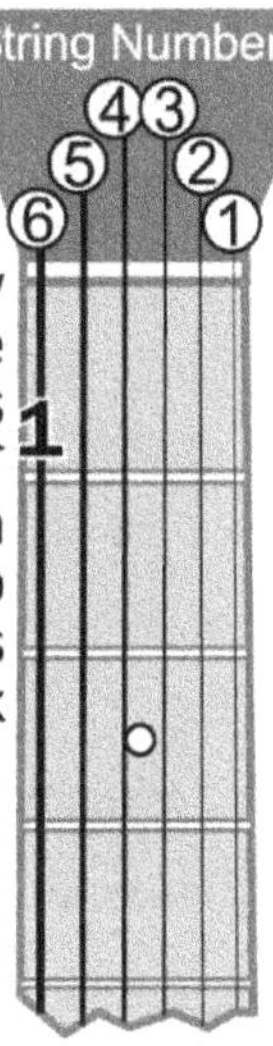

Add Finger 2 — Leave **Finger 1** in place as you play this note 8 times

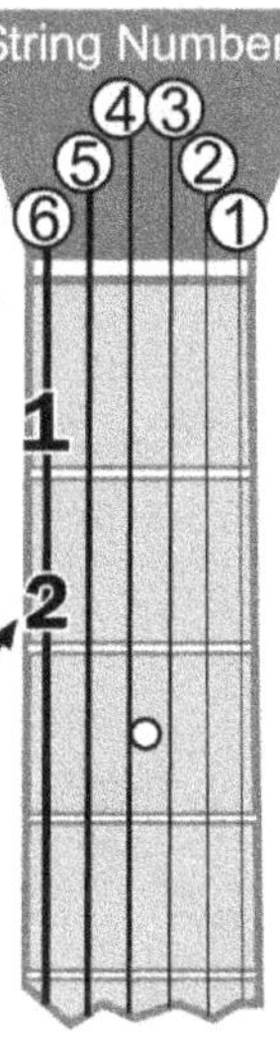

Add Finger 3 — Leave **Fingers 1 & 2** in place as you play this note 8 times

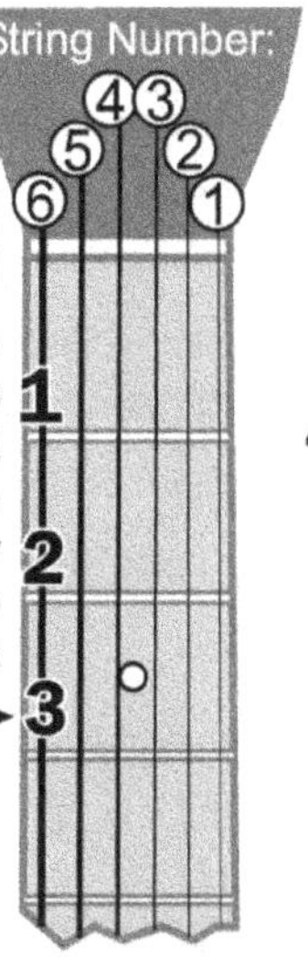

Add Finger 4 — All **4 Fingers** should stay on the neck as you play this note 8 times

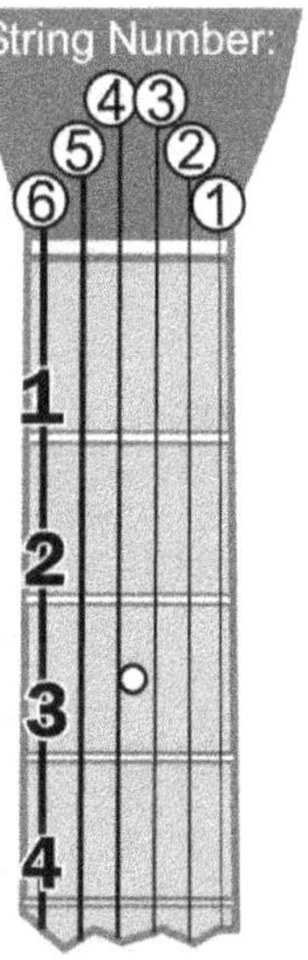

Repeat the 32 note sequence as described above on **String 5**.

Do the same on **Strings 4, 3, 2 & 1** going across the neck.

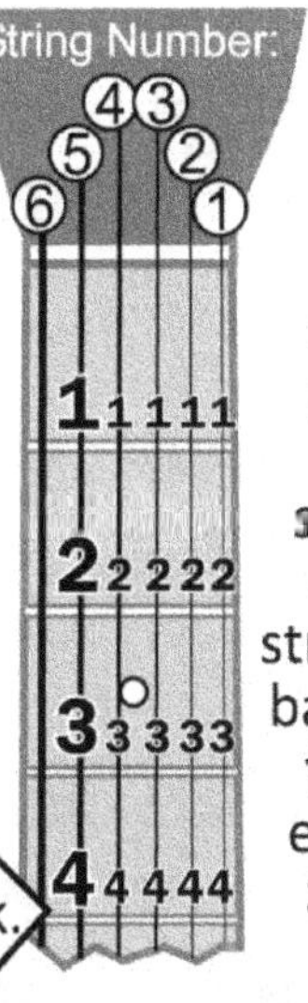

From **String 1** play the 32 note sequence on each string again, back across the neck ending on **String 6**.

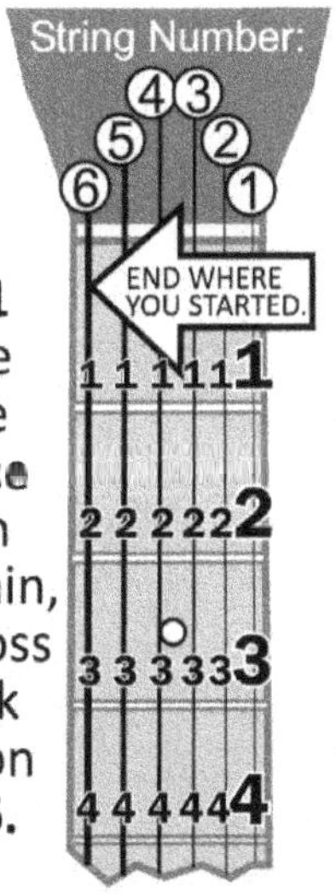

END WHERE YOU STARTED.

Count the 8 notes on each fret: 1-2-3-4...1-2-3-4.

Use the rebounding technique described on page 72 to develop even, accurate picking.

Gradually develop speed. Maintain precise, even picking. Do not sacrifice precison for speed.

Using the hand position described on page 73 will make this exercise easier to perform.

The Tremolo Exercise is presented on the following pages in Standard Notation and TAB.

TREMOLO

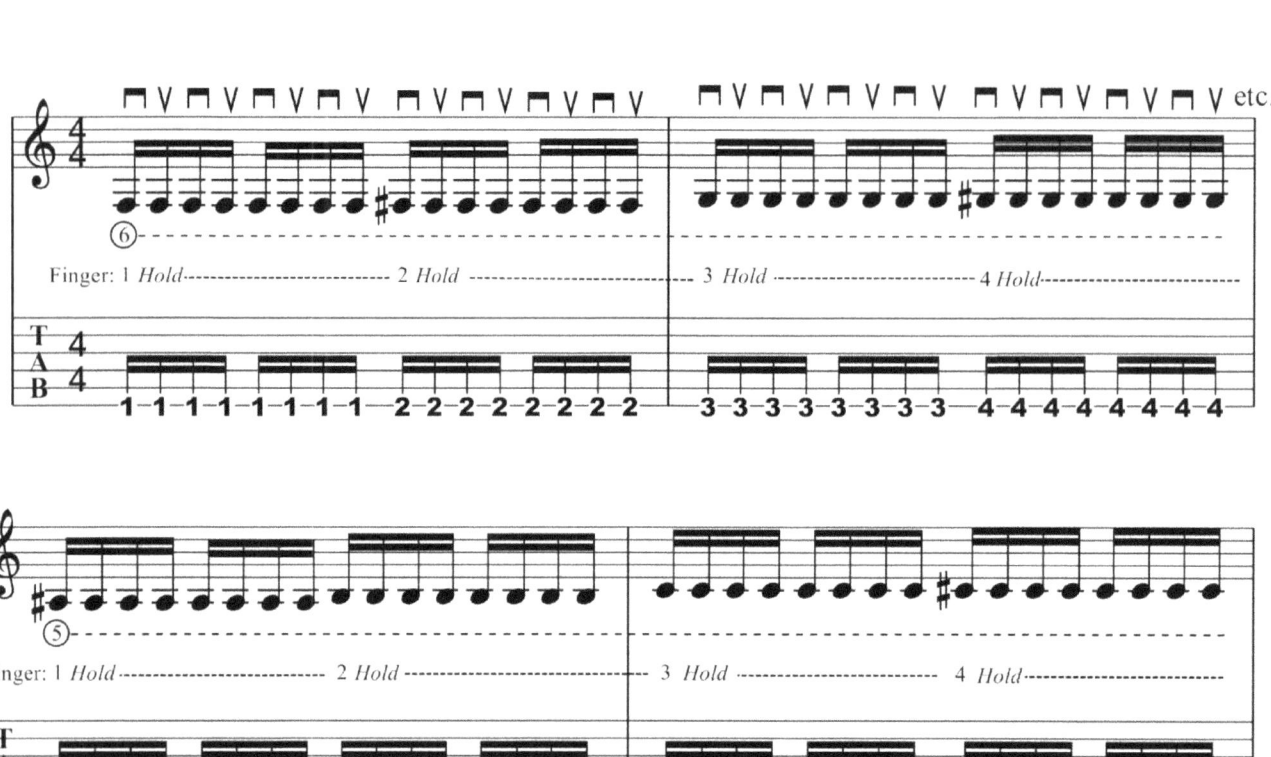
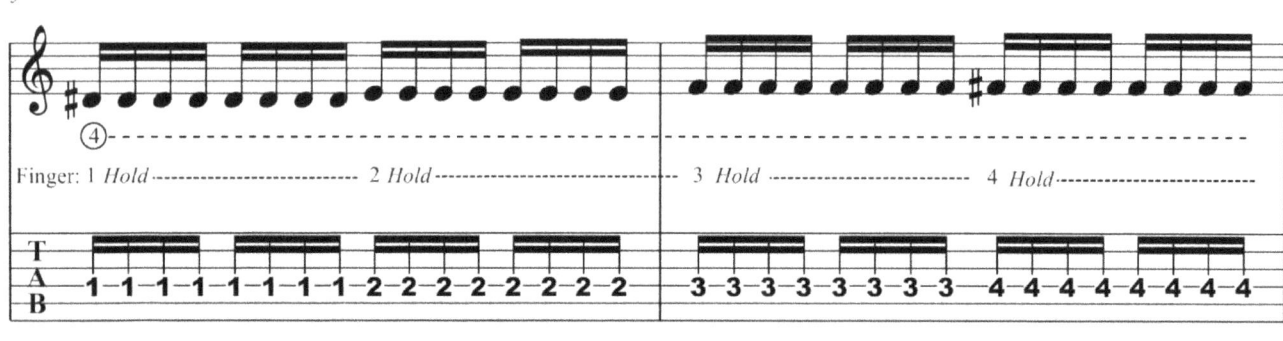
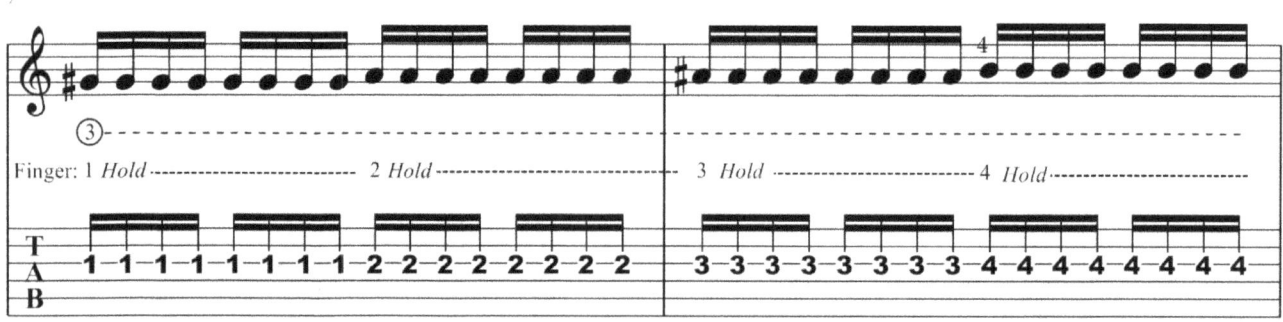

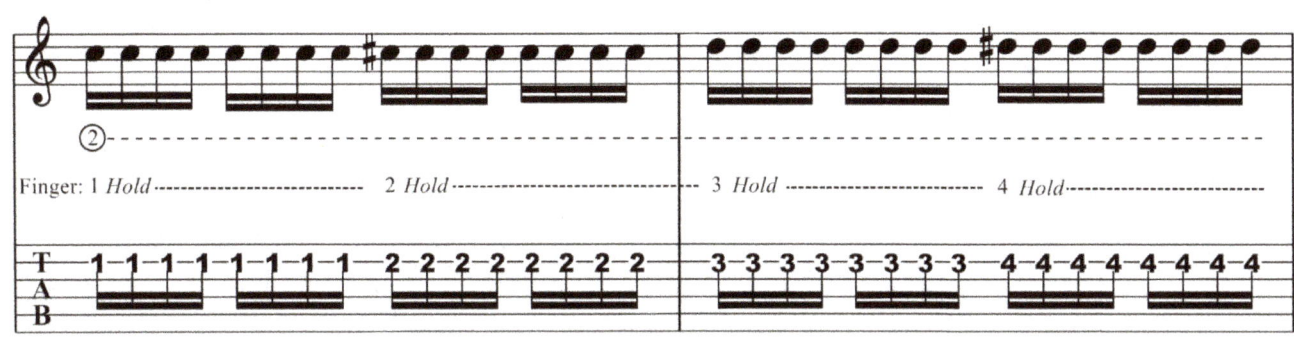
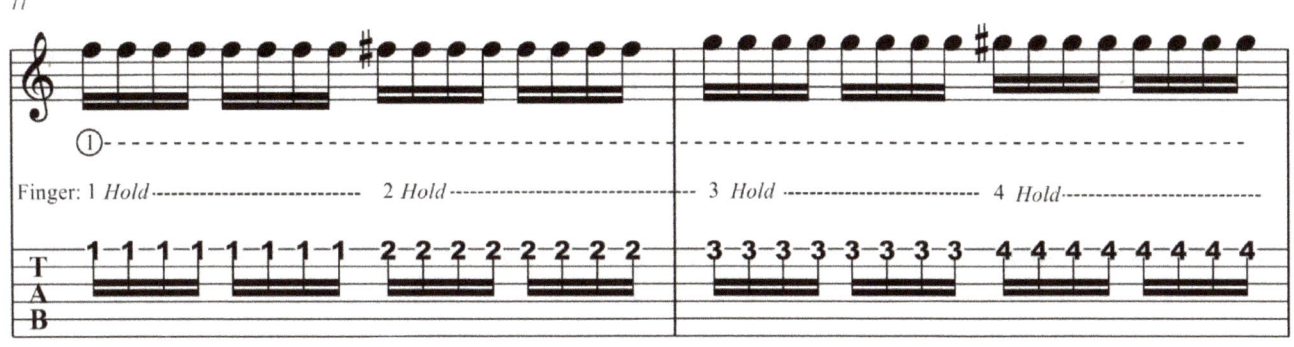
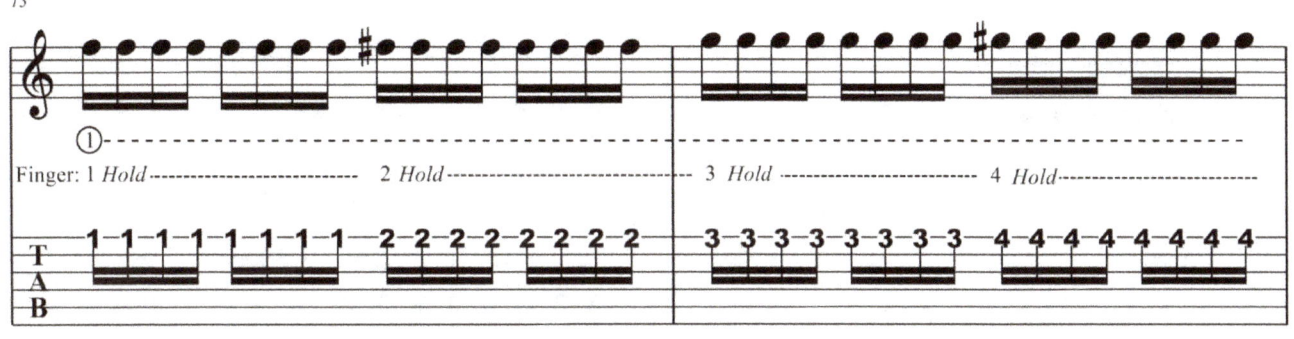
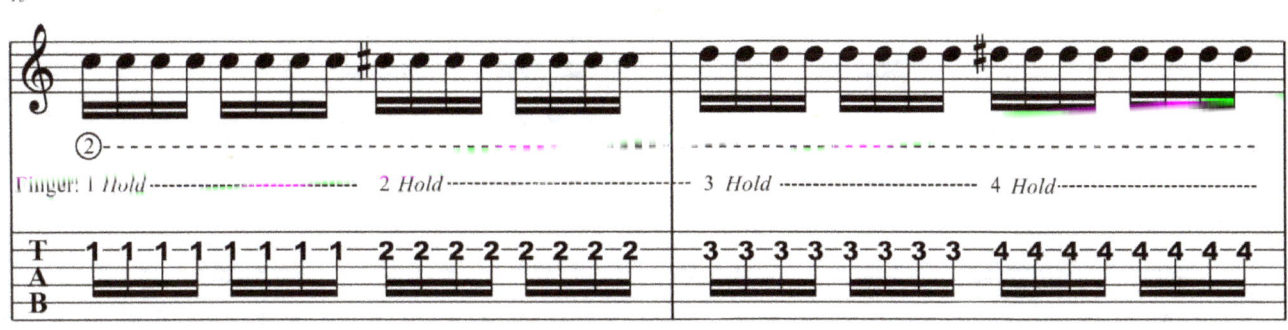

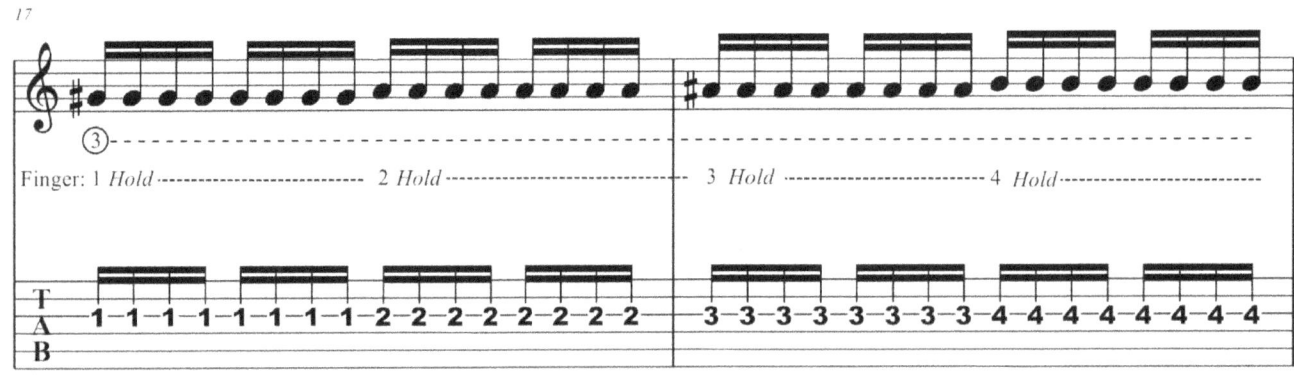
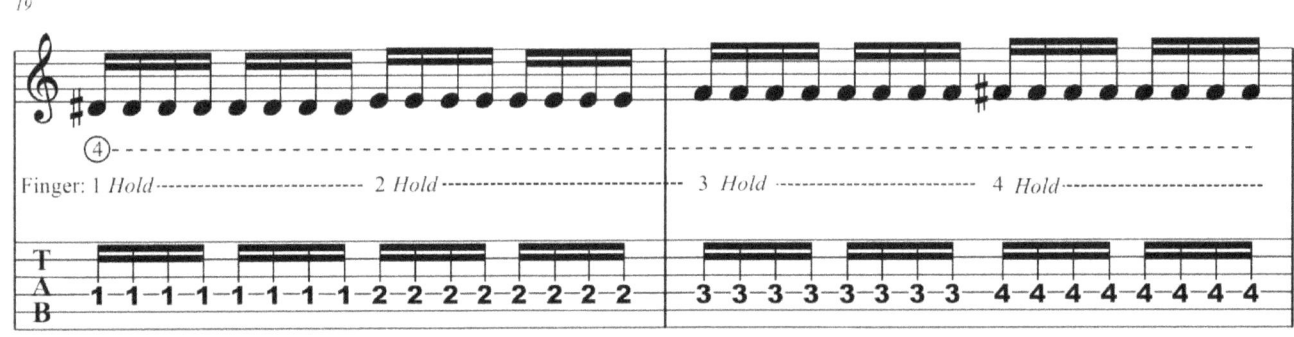
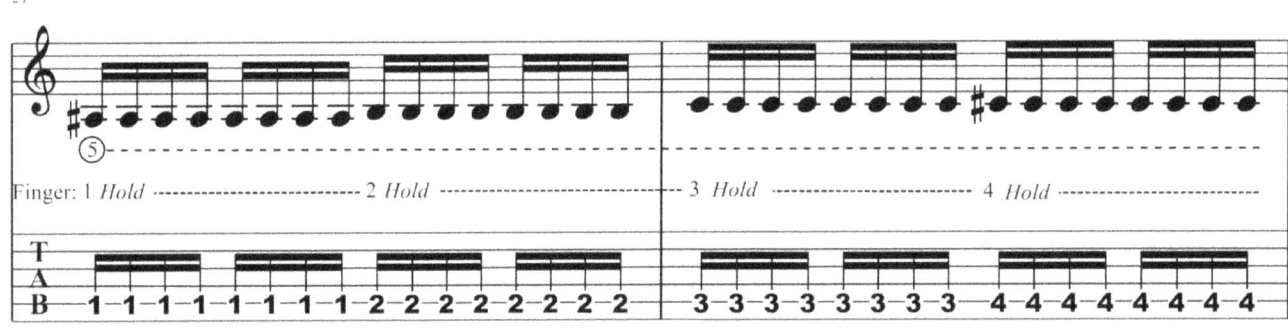
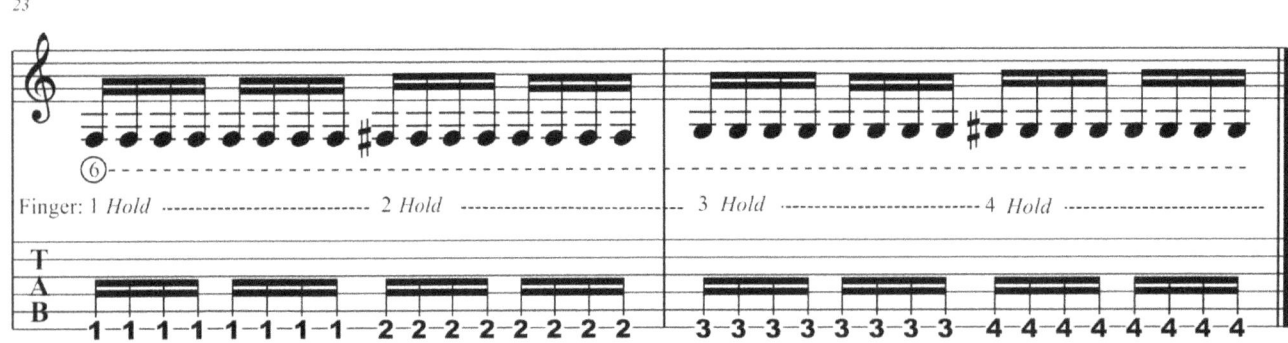

2. FINGER EXERCISE

Develops dexterity and strength in all fingers of the LEFT HAND.
Fosters precision picking with the RIGHT HAND.

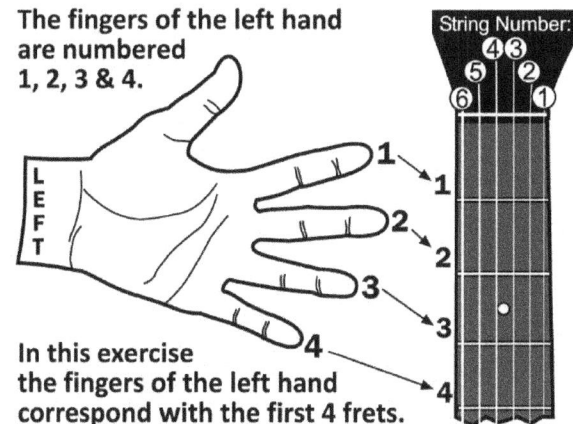

The fingers of the left hand are numbered 1, 2, 3 & 4.

In this exercise the fingers of the left hand correspond with the first 4 frets.

The Finger Excercise consists of 2 note combinations played on each string twice.

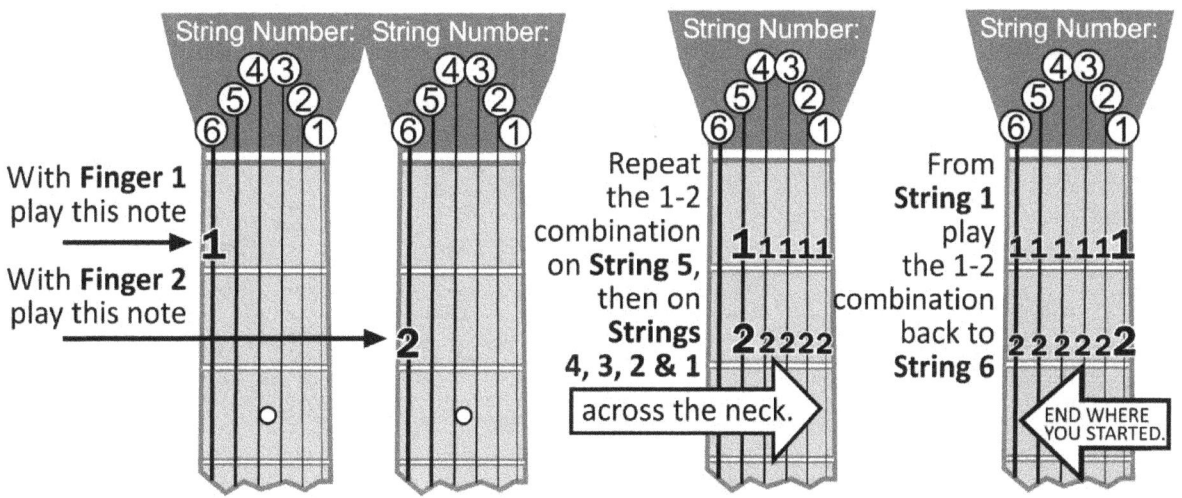

With **Finger 1** play this note
With **Finger 2** play this note

Repeat the 1-2 combination on **String 5**, then on **Strings 4, 3, 2 & 1** across the neck.

From **String 1** play the 1-2 combination back to **String 6**. END WHERE YOU STARTED.

Play these 2 note combinations twice on each string as described above.

1-2	2-1
1-3	3-1
1-4	4-1
2-3	3-2
2-4	4-2
3-4	4-3

> Pick slowly and evenly, using Down and Up strokes.
>
> Use the picking technique learned in the previous TREMOLO exercise.
>
> Gradually develop speed, while maintaining precise, even picking.
>
> Repeat the exercise using Up-Down picking.
>
> Beginners should pick with all downstrokes at first.

The Finger Exercise is presented on the following pages in Standard Notation and TAB.

FINGER EXERCISE

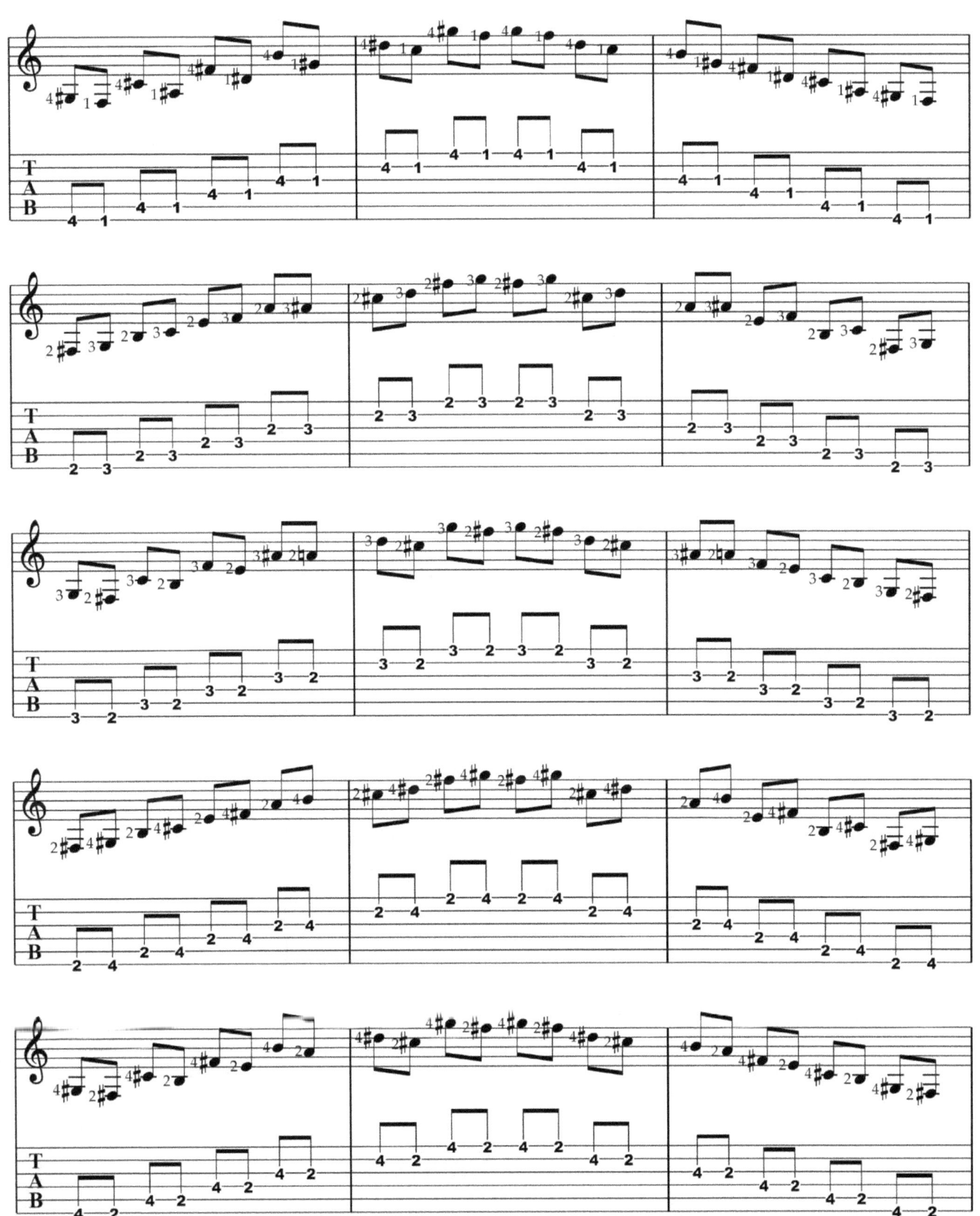

Repeat the exercise using Up-Down picking.

> It is suggested that
> as you learn each exercise
> that you do each daily
> so that eventually
> all sections together
> form the complete
> warm-up period.

3. SHIFT EXERCISE

Develops ease and accuracy moving the LEFT HAND up the guitar neck from fret to fret.

The fingers of the left hand are numbered 1, 2, 3 & 4.

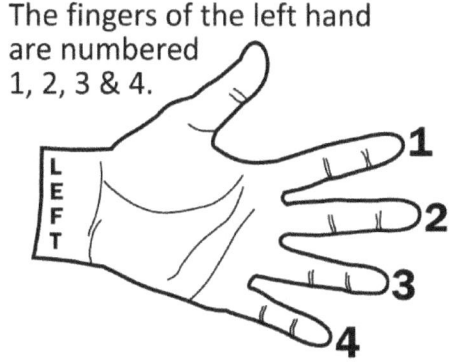

The Shift Excercise is a repeating 8 note sequence that shifts from one fret to the next sliding up the guitar neck.

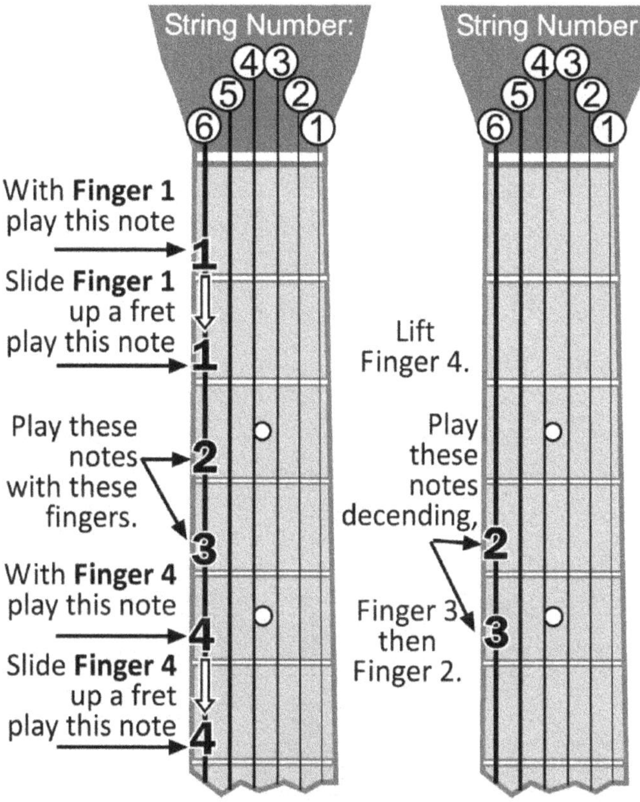

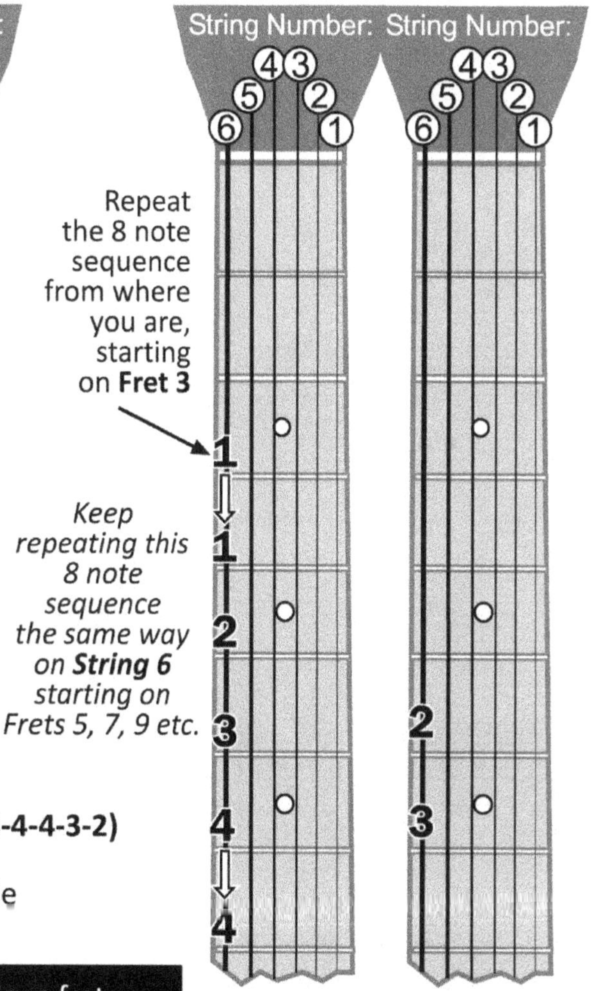

With **Finger 1** play this note

Slide **Finger 1** up a fret play this note

Play these notes with these fingers.

With **Finger 4** play this note

Slide **Finger 4** up a fret play this note

Lift Finger 4.

Play these notes decending,

Finger 3 then Finger 2.

Repeat the 8 note sequence from where you are, starting on **Fret 3**

*Keep repeating this 8 note sequence the same way on **String 6** starting on Frets 5, 7, 9 etc.*

Play the repeating 8 Note Sequence (1-1-2-3-4-4-3-2) on ALL SIX STRINGS.
Go up the neck as far as is comfortable on your particular guitar.

You don't have to hold each note on the previous frets, but keep the LEFT HAND finger tips close to the strings.

Play slowly and evenly, gradually build up speed.

Use DOWN & UP picking.

Repeat the full exercise with UP & DOWN picking.

The Shift Exercise is presented on the following pages in Standard Notation and TAB.

SHIFT EXERCISE

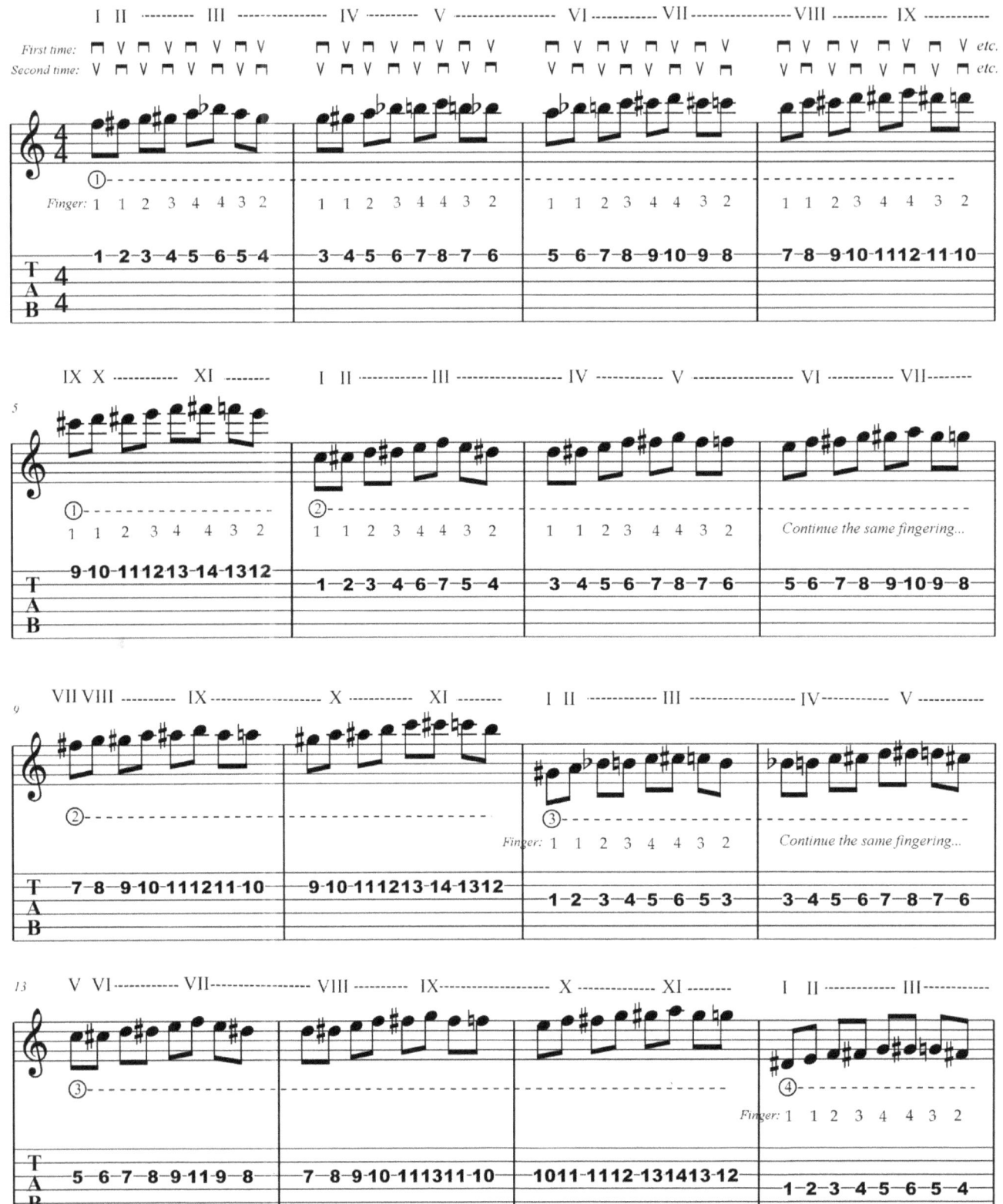

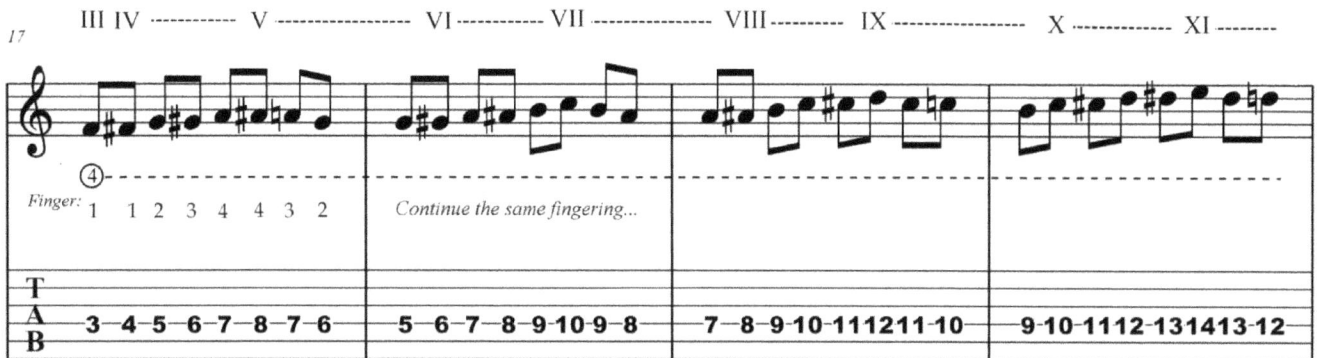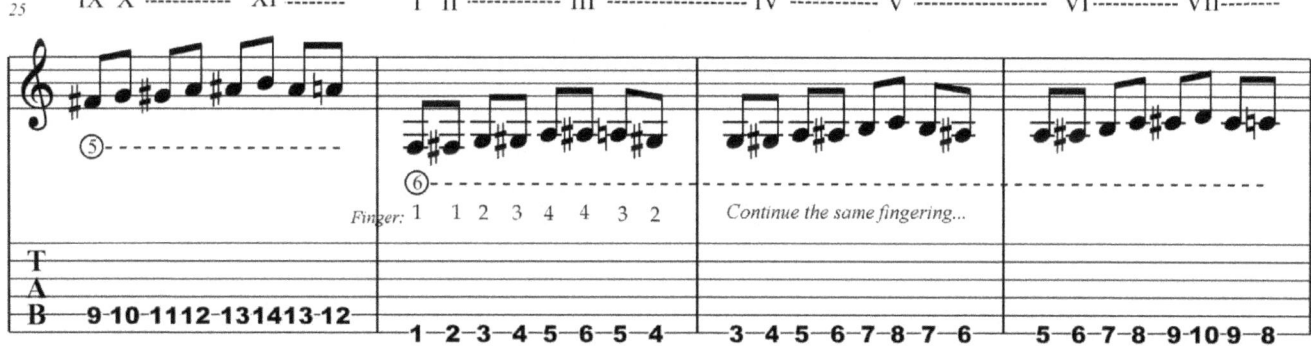

Repeat exercise with Up-Down picking

> Players have many methods
> as to when to apply
> down and up picking.
> Nothing can account for
> every type of melody
> that we come across.
> However, the suggestions
> in this book are consistent and
> lay down a sound foundation
> for coping with various types
> of melodic figurations.

4. BACKPICKING

Develops precise control moving the RIGHT HAND from string to string.
Also develops accuracy in the LEFT HAND sliding chords from fret to fret.

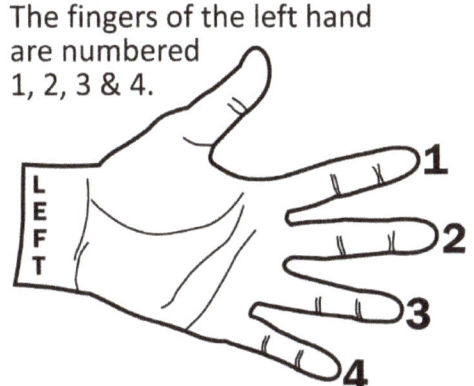

The fingers of the left hand are numbered 1, 2, 3 & 4.

The Backpicking Exercise consists of 4 note chords played as individual notes. The exercise is performed in 3 parts on 3 different string groups.

Beginners should practice the picking technique on open strings until holding a 4 note chord is comfortable.

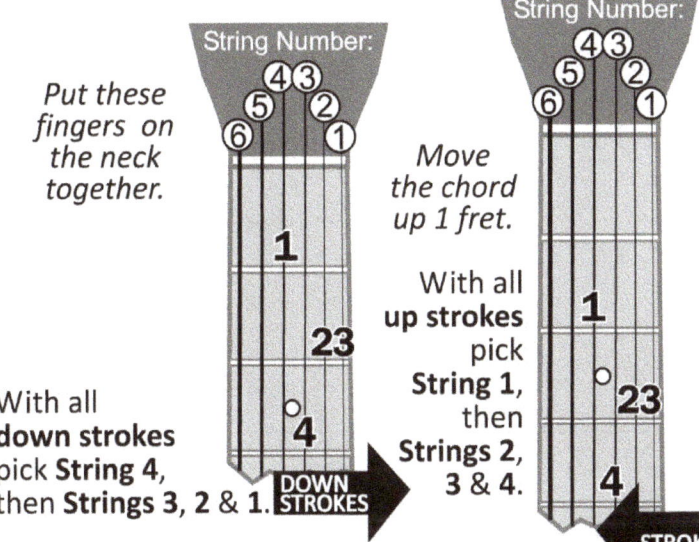

Put these fingers on the neck together.

With all **down strokes** pick **String 4**, then **Strings 3, 2 & 1**.

Move the chord up 1 fret.

With all **up strokes** pick **String 1**, then **Strings 2, 3 & 4**.

Continue up the neck, moving the chord one fret at a time, picking with 4 downstrokes then 4 upstrokes.

Go up the neck as far as possible on your guitar.

GO SLOWLY & EVENLY.
Each note should be perfectly spaced apart and plucked with identical force.

PART 2
Put the same chord on **Strings 2, 3, 4, & 5**.
Repeat the exercise as described above.

PART 3
Put the same chord on **Strings 3, 4, 5, & 6**.
Repeat the exercise as described above.

DO NOT STRUM as you would playing a chord. All four notes of each chord should be heard distinctly, as separate notes.

Count the notes: 1-2-3-4

Do not sacrifice precison for speed, each note must be evenly spaced and plucked with identical attack.

Once perfected, backpicking yields a **harplike effect**. This technique allows the player to perform any chord as an arpeggio on the guitar.

The Backpicking Exercise is presented on the following pages in Standard Notation and TAB.

BACKPICKING

PART 2

PART 3

5. ALTERNATE PICKING

Develops precise control with the RIGHT HAND skipping over strings while maintaining accurate and even picking. Also develops accuracy in the LEFT HAND moving chords up the neck from fret to fret.

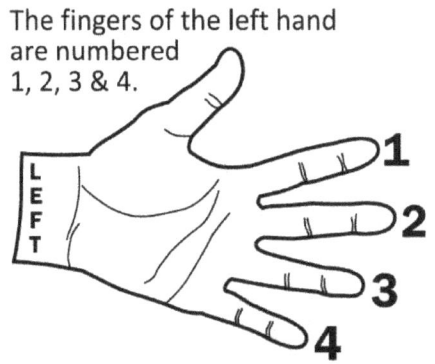

The fingers of the left hand are numbered 1, 2, 3 & 4.

Alternate Picking is a 2 part exercise consisting of 4 note chords played as individual notes. The 2 parts feature different picking patterns. The 2 parts are performed in 3 sections on different string groups.

Beginners should practice the picking technique on open strings until holding the 4 note chord is comfortable.

PART 1

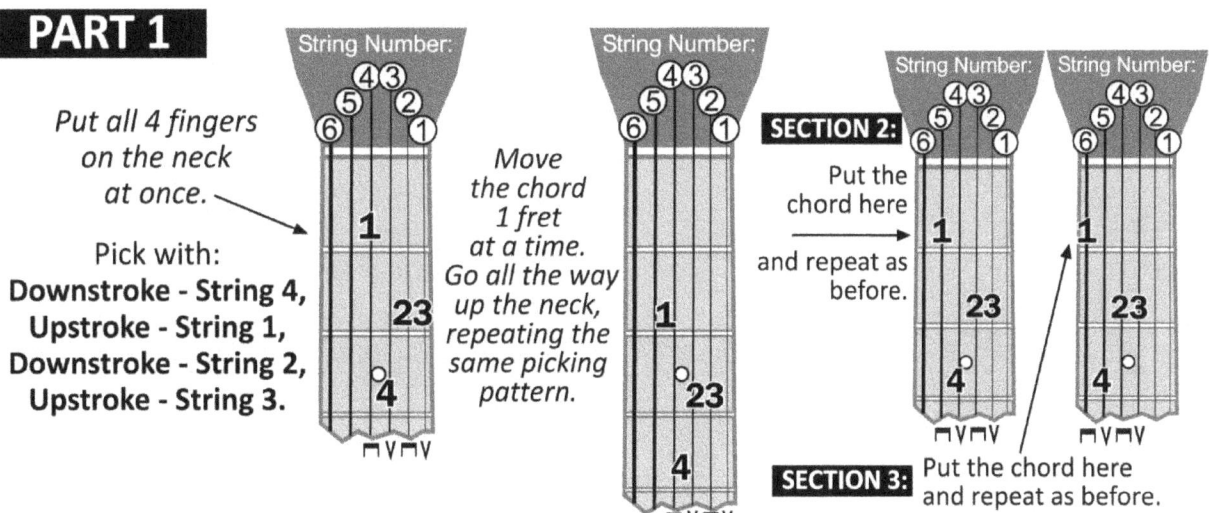

Put all 4 fingers on the neck at once.

Pick with:
**Downstroke - String 4,
Upstroke - String 1,
Downstroke - String 2,
Upstroke - String 3.**

Move the chord 1 fret at a time. Go all the way up the neck, repeating the same picking pattern.

SECTION 2: Put the chord here and repeat as before.

SECTION 3: Put the chord here and repeat as before.

PART 2

Perform the same as Part 1 but with a new picking pattern.

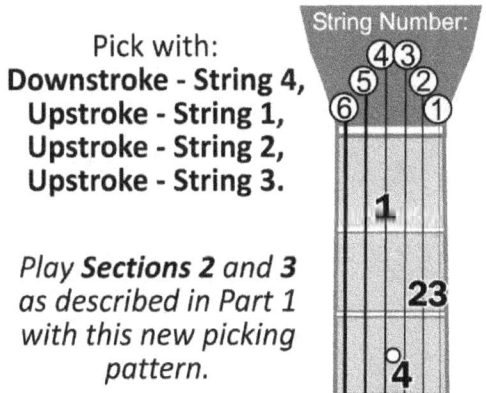

Pick with:
**Downstroke - String 4,
Upstroke - String 1,
Upstroke - String 2,
Upstroke - String 3.**

*Play **Sections 2** and **3** as described in Part 1 with this new picking pattern.*

Hold the chord using your fingertips, this will make sliding the chord up the neck easier.

Go slowly and evenly.

DO NOT SACRIFICE PRECISION FOR SPEED, each note should be evenly spaced and plucked with identical attack.

The Alternate Picking Exercise is presented on the following pages in Standard Notation and TAB.

ALTERNATE PICKING

SECTION 2

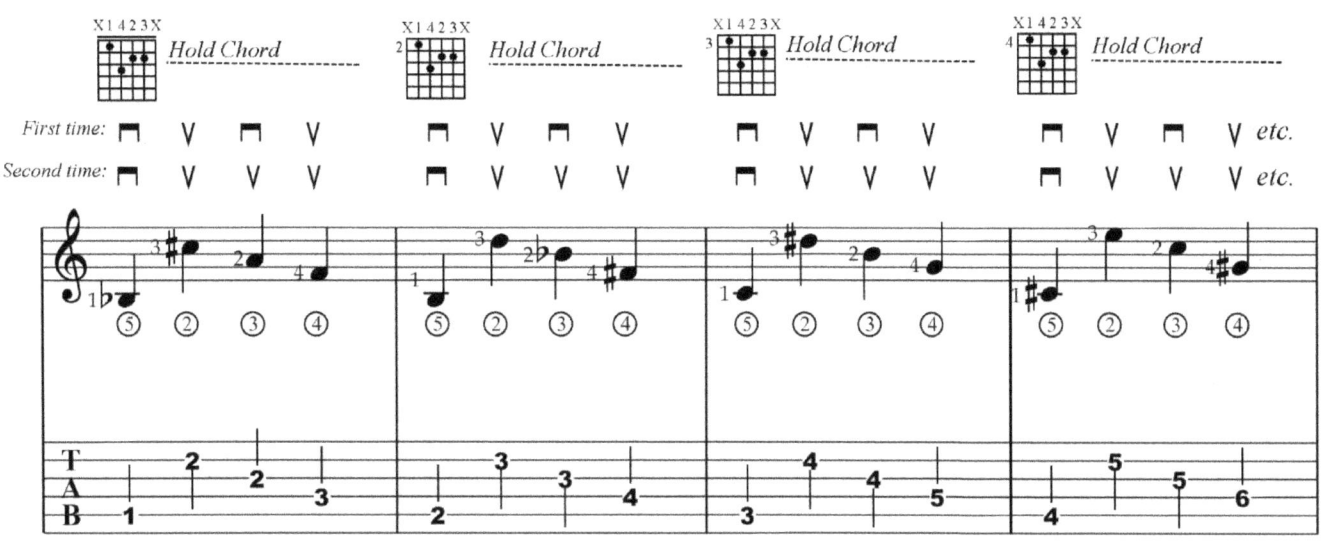
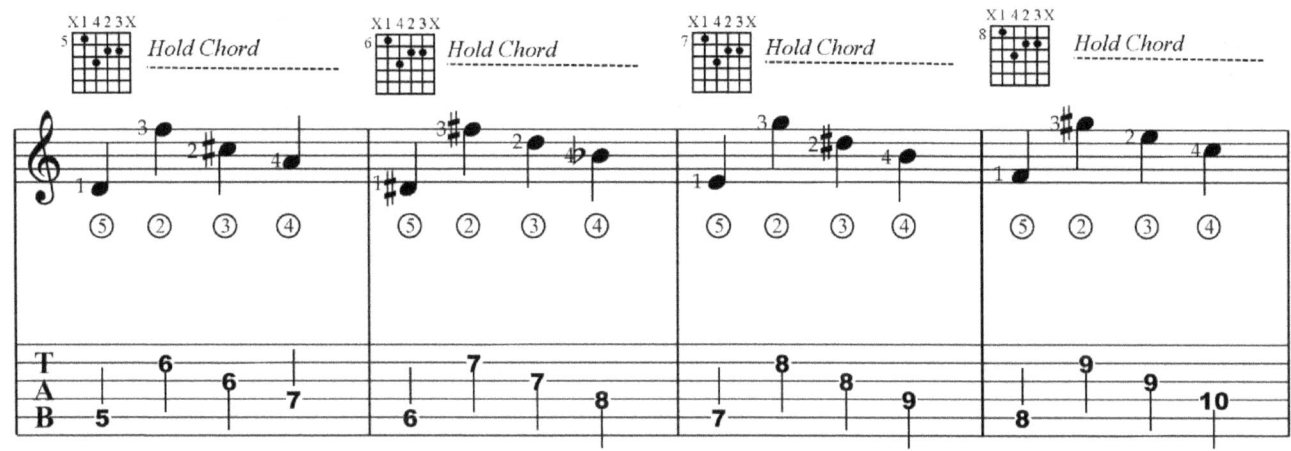
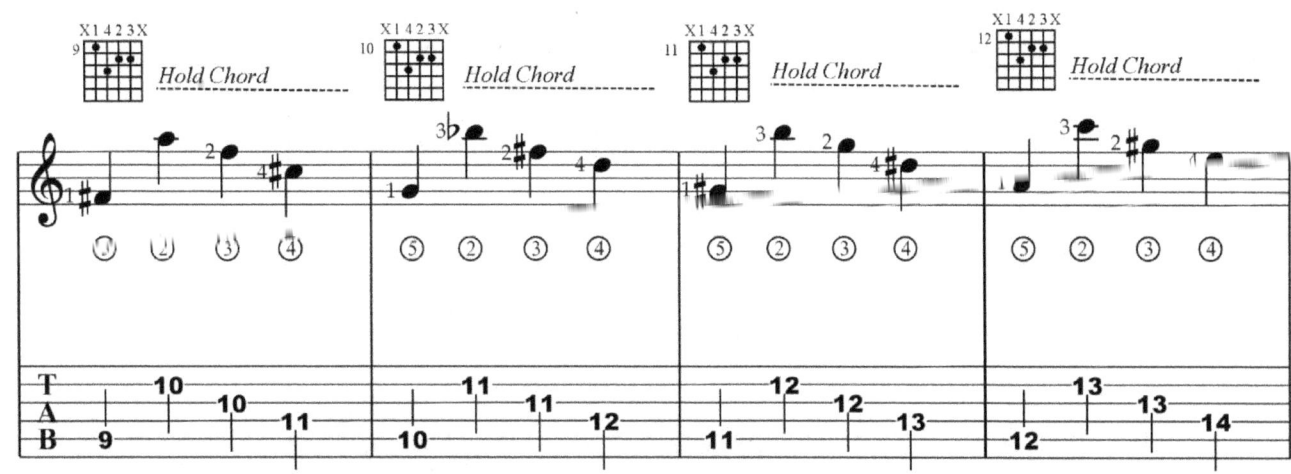

SECTION 3

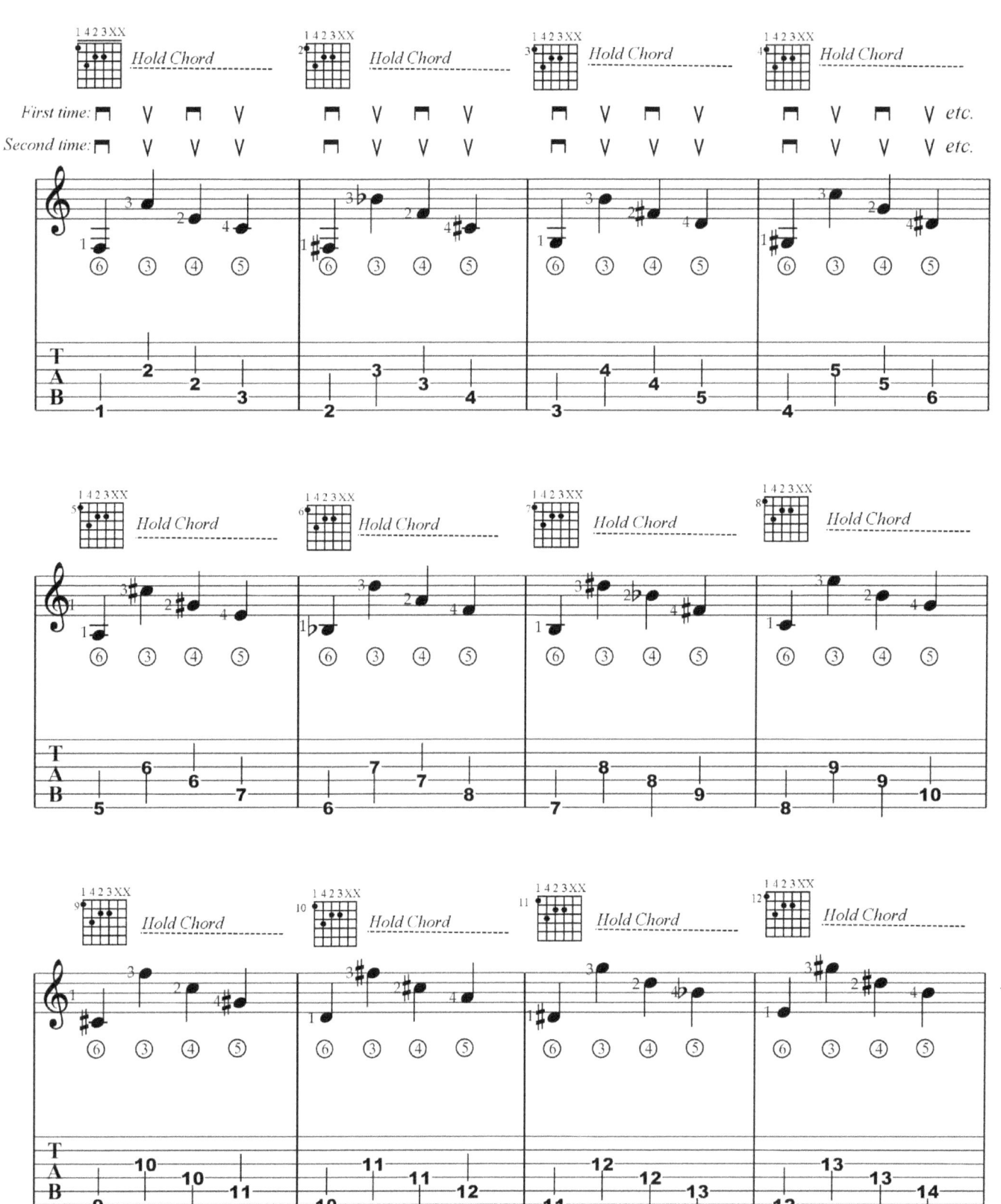

Repeat full exercise with 2nd picking style.

6. CROSS PICKING

Develops precise control with the RIGHT HAND skipping over multiple strings while maintaining accurate and even picking. Also develops accuracy in the LEFT HAND moving INTERVALS (2 note pairs) up the neck from fret to fret.

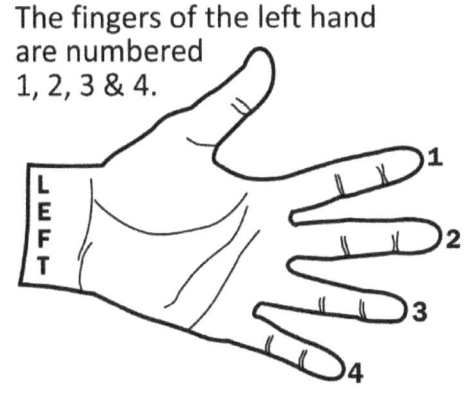

The fingers of the left hand are numbered 1, 2, 3 & 4.

The Cross Picking Exercise consists of 2 note sequences (intervals) played as individual notes moving up the neck. There are 5 parts to the exercise, each played on different string groups.

This exercise uses all natural notes on the guitar, no sharps or flats.

*For convenience
and easier continuity,
the instructional diagrams
for this exercise
are presented on the
following 2 facing pages.*

⟶

**Use the pairs of intervals below.
In each interval, put both fingers on the neck at once,
then pick the interval as individual notes.**

**With downstrokes & upstrokes
play the patterns up the neck shown on the facing page.**

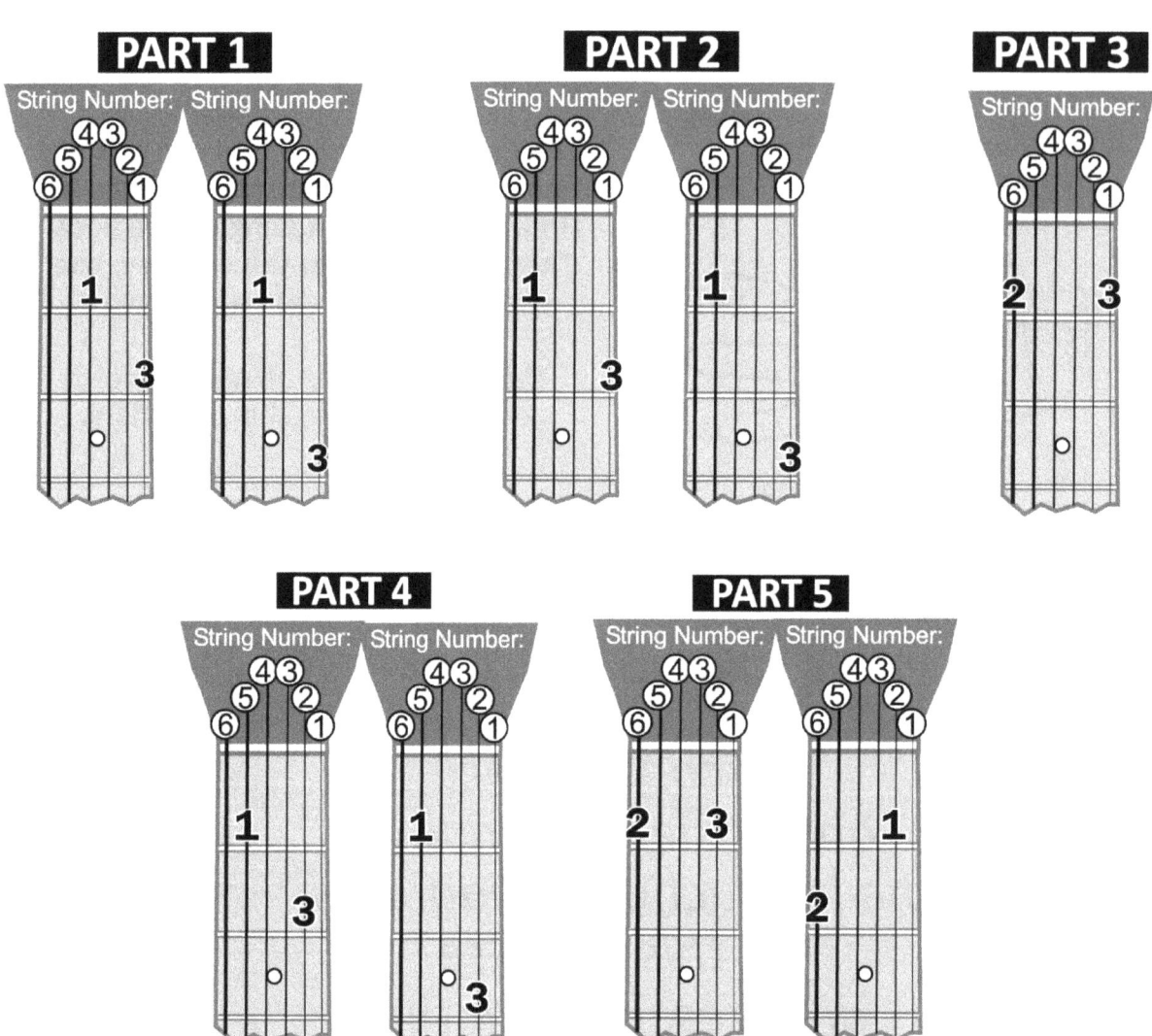

**Once you place the 2 fingers down
DO NOT LIFT THEM UP.**

**SLIDE each 2 note interval up the neck. Take care to maintain the fingers
on the proper frets as you slide.**

Hold the interval with your fingertips, that will make it easier to slide.

Play each interval twice as single notes. Count 1-2-3-4.
Slide each interval up the neck to the frets shown below.

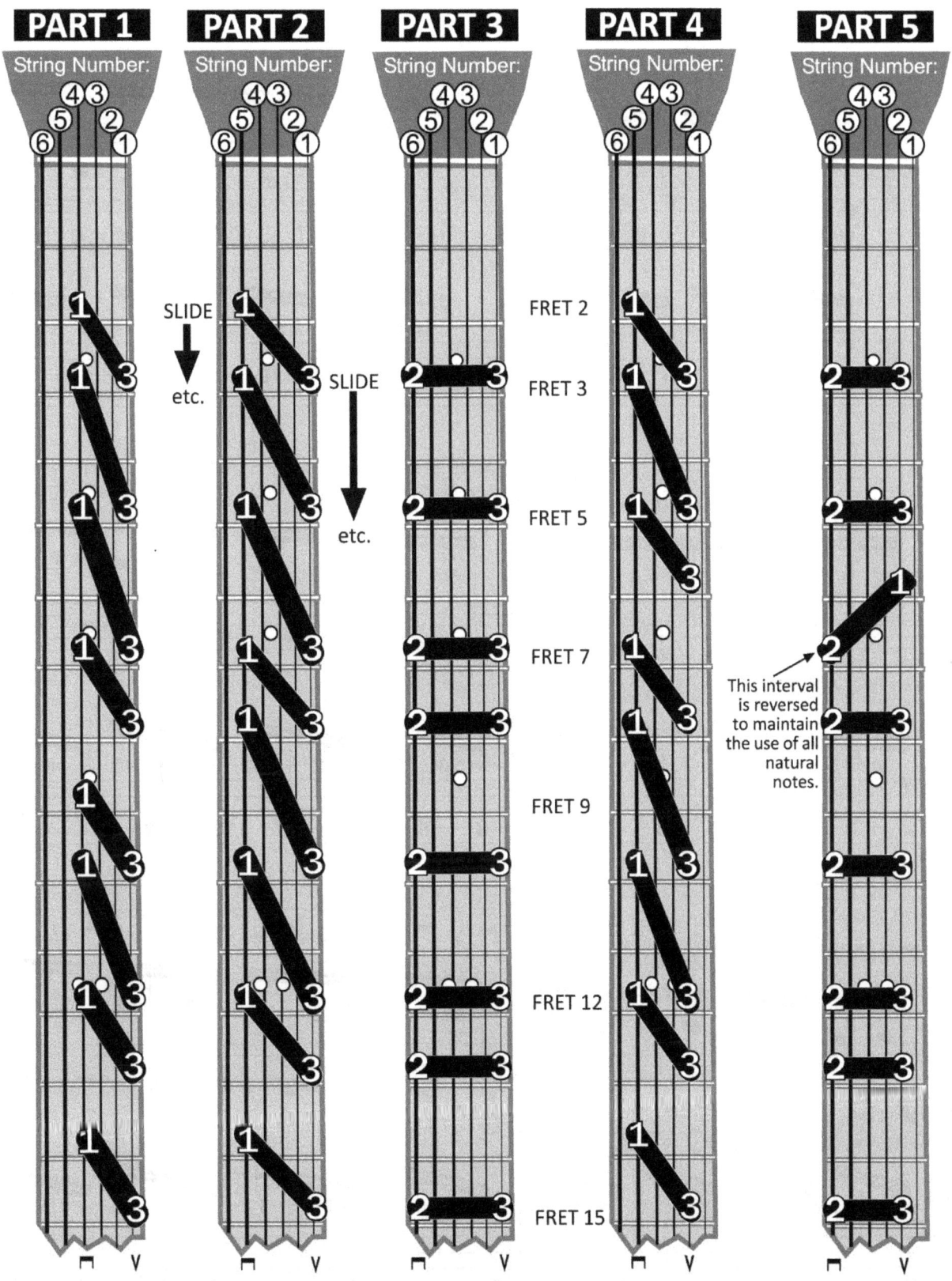

The Cross Picking Exercise is presented on the following pages in Standard Notation and TAB.

CROSS PICKING

PART 1

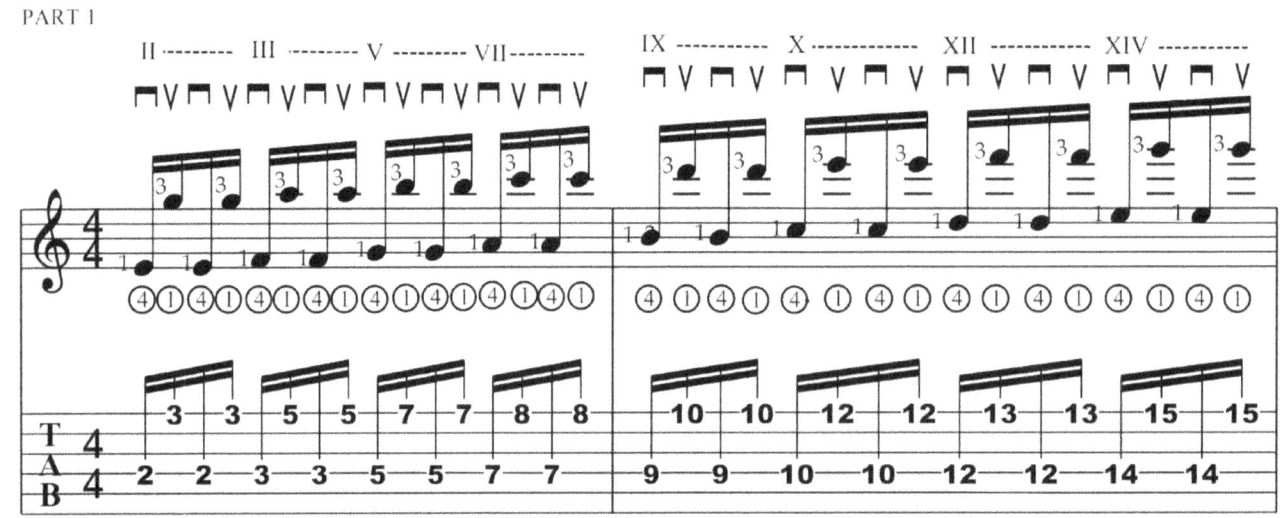

PART 2

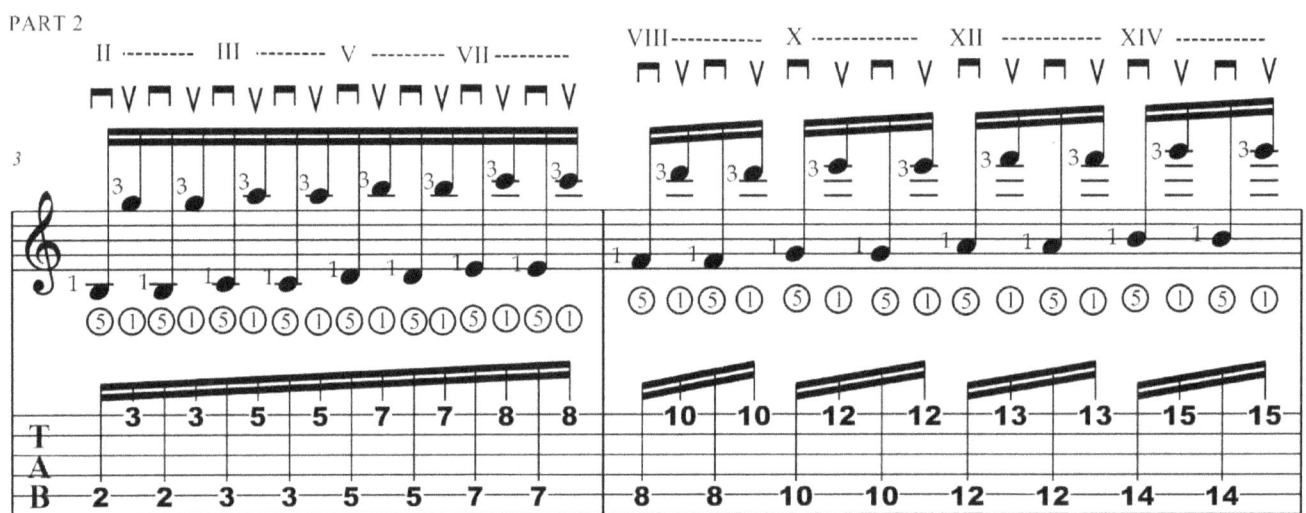

PART 3

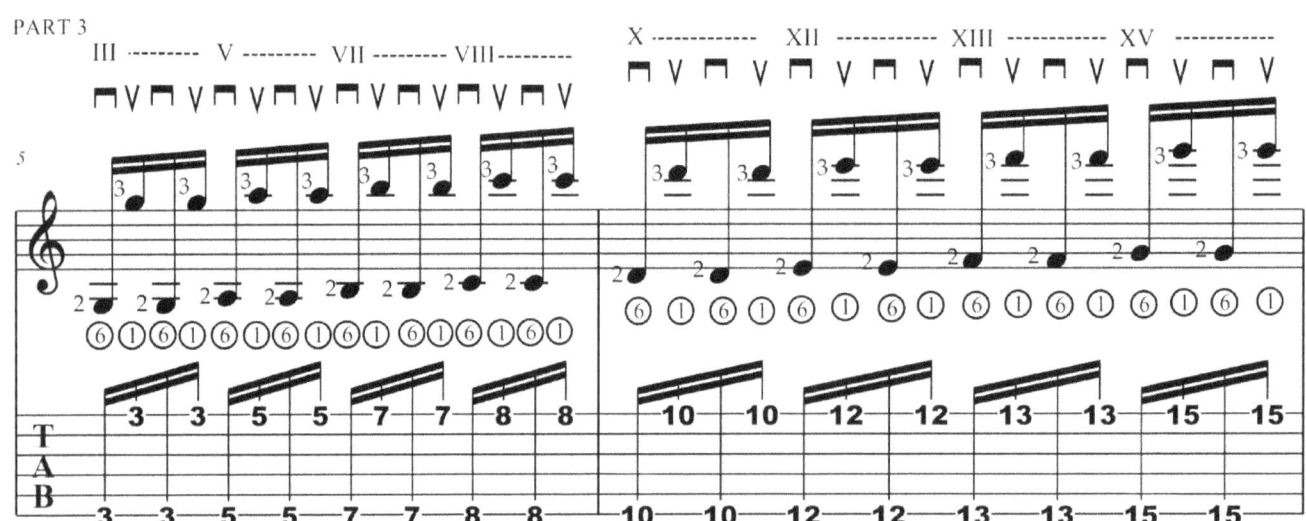

Go as far up the neck as is comfortable on your guitar.

PART 4

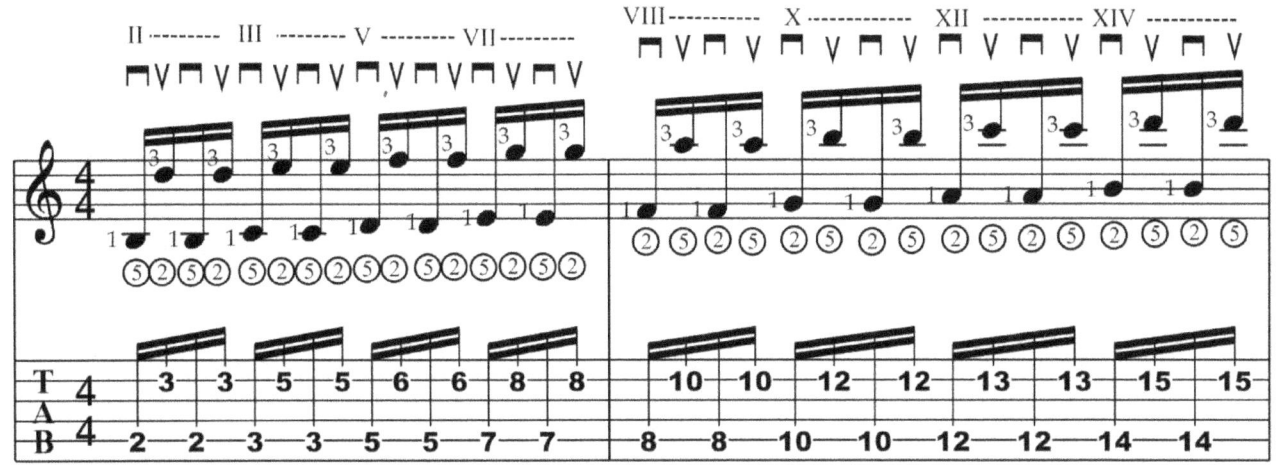

PART 5

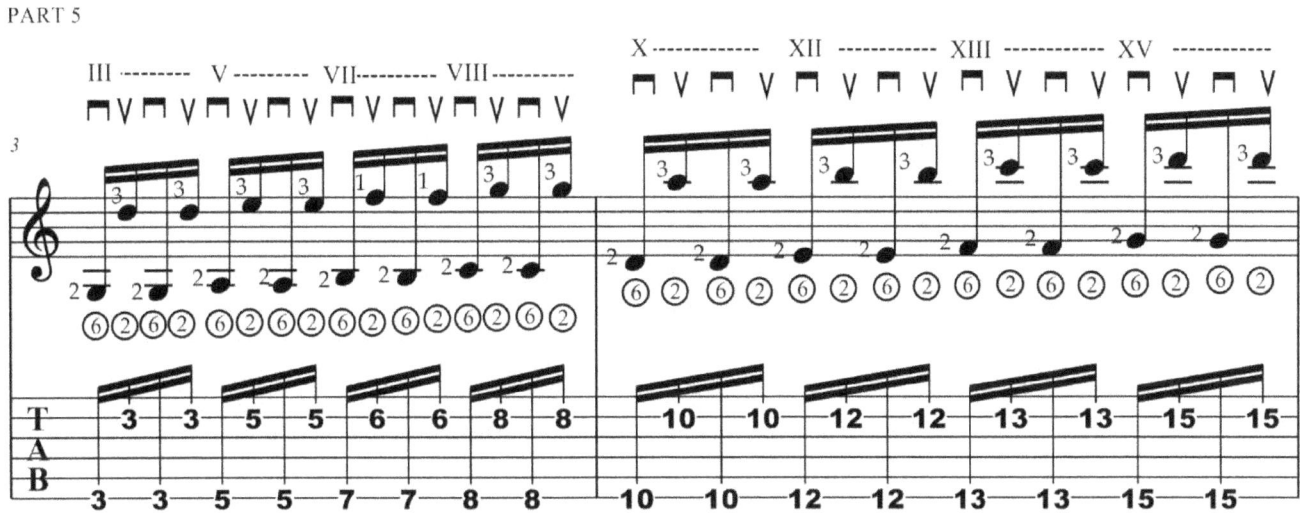

Go as far up the neck as is comfortable on your guitar.

Decending arpeggios usually
present an obstacle to players
because of having to control
up picks in succession.
It is suggested to closely imitate
the motion of the down pick
when learning and
practicing up picks.

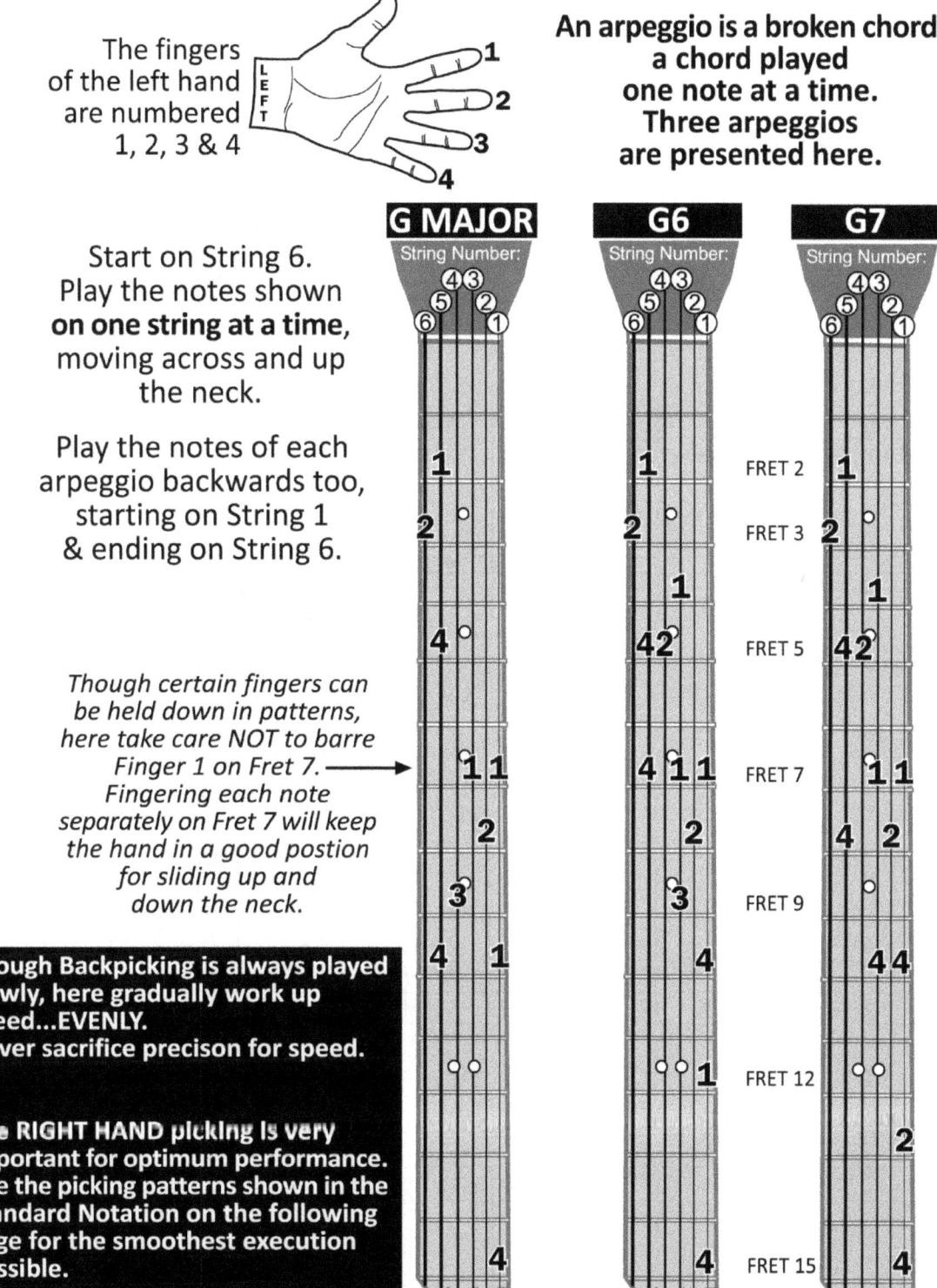

ARPEGGIO

G7

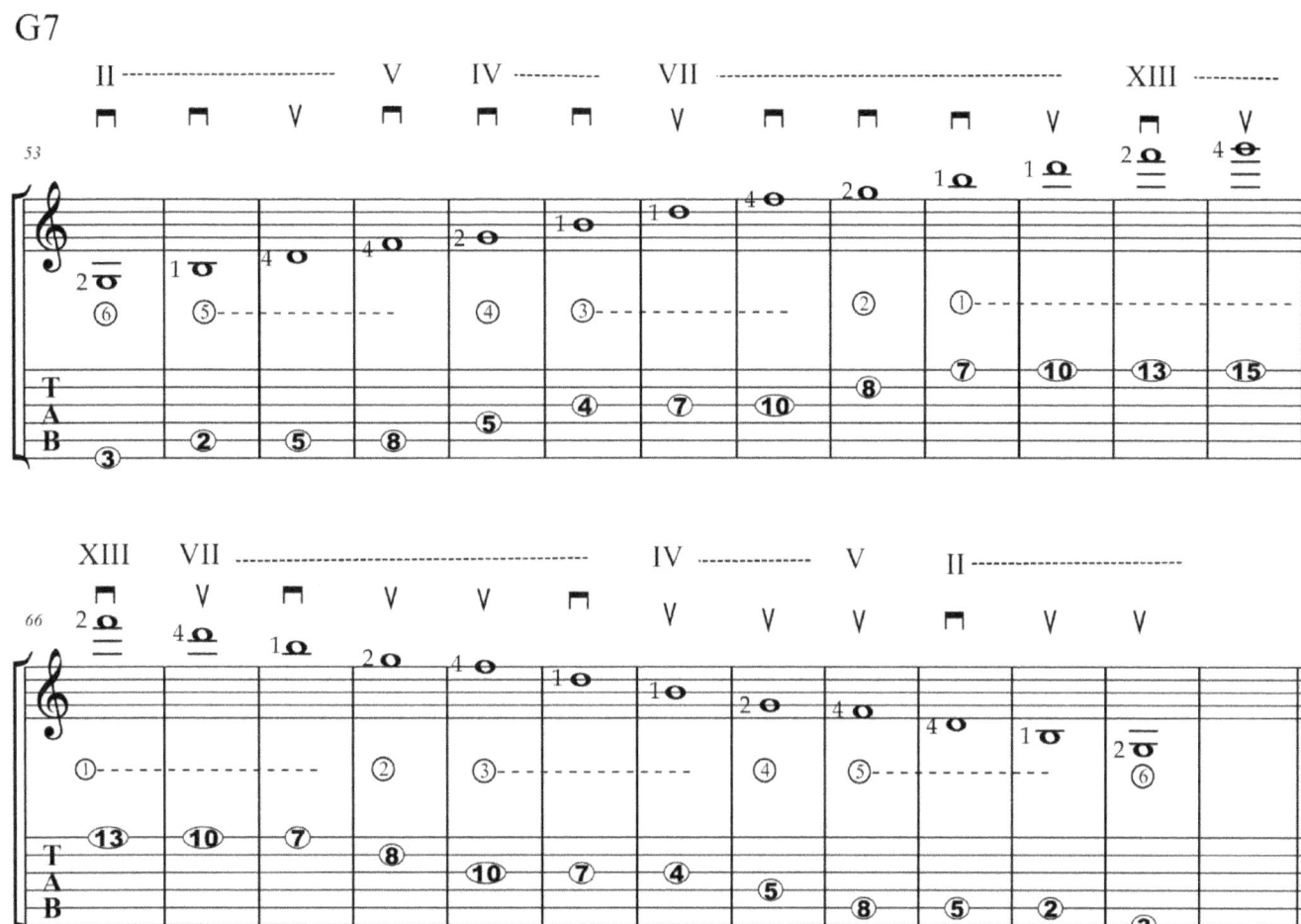

> Success with the Barre Exercise may also be affected by the action of the guitar, that is the height of the strings from the finger board. It is best to use a guitar with the easiest action possible. The Barre Exercise is not a muscle building exercise.

8. BARRE EXERCISES

Develops the ability in the LEFT HAND to hold multiple notes simultaneously with one finger. Develops the strength and stamina to play Barre Chords and the dexterity to play single note passages featuring barred fingering.

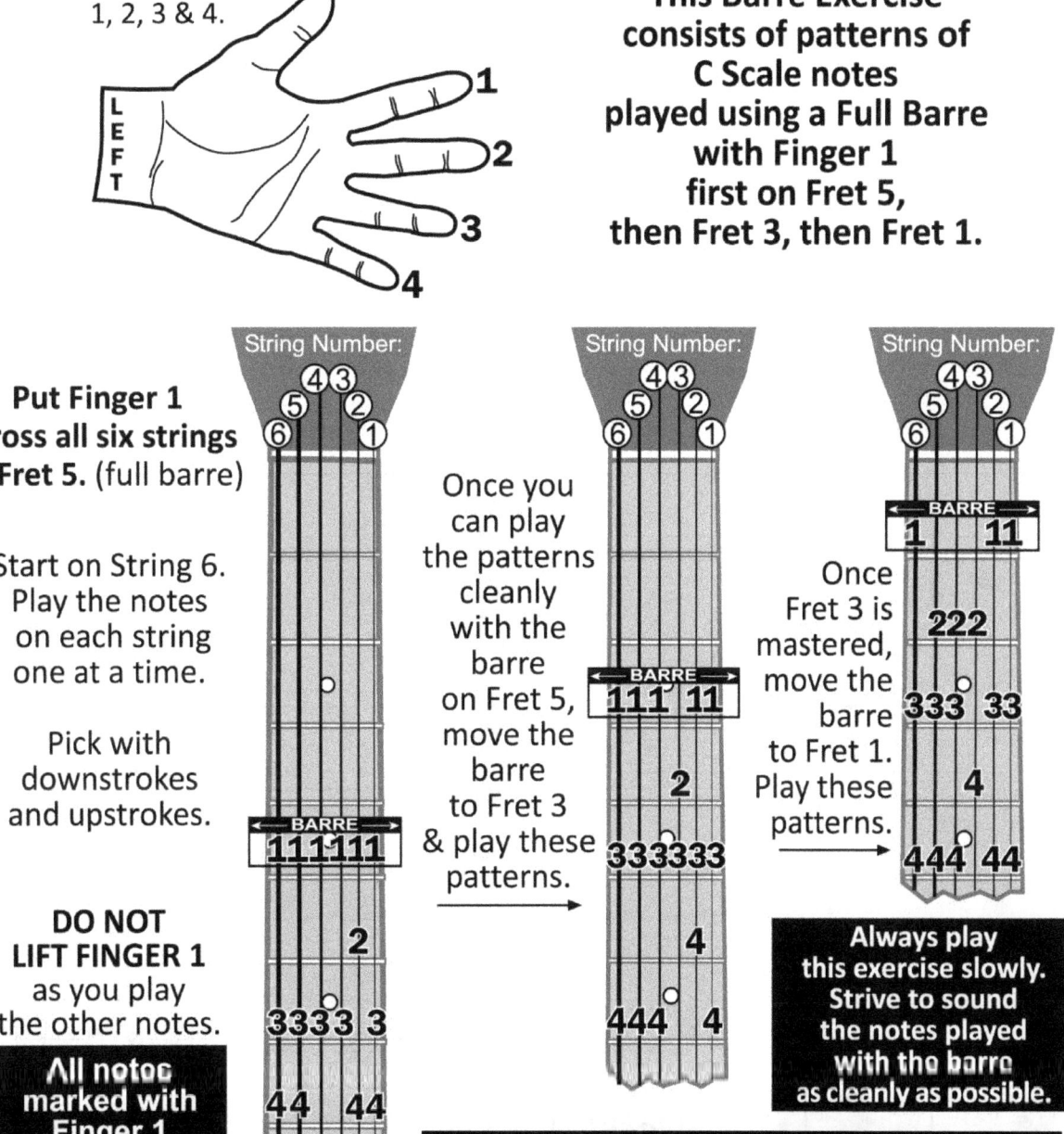

BARRE EXERCISE
All "1" fingerings are played with the barre.

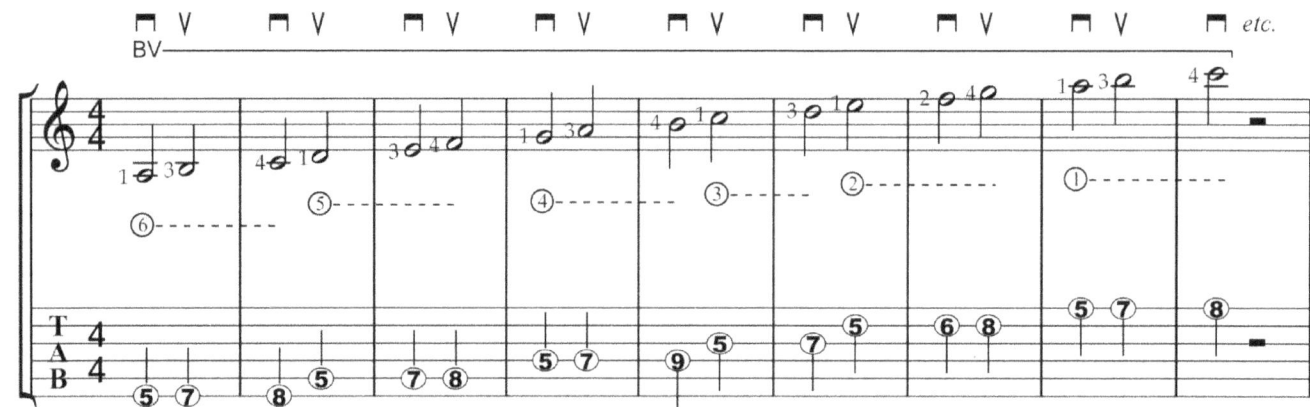
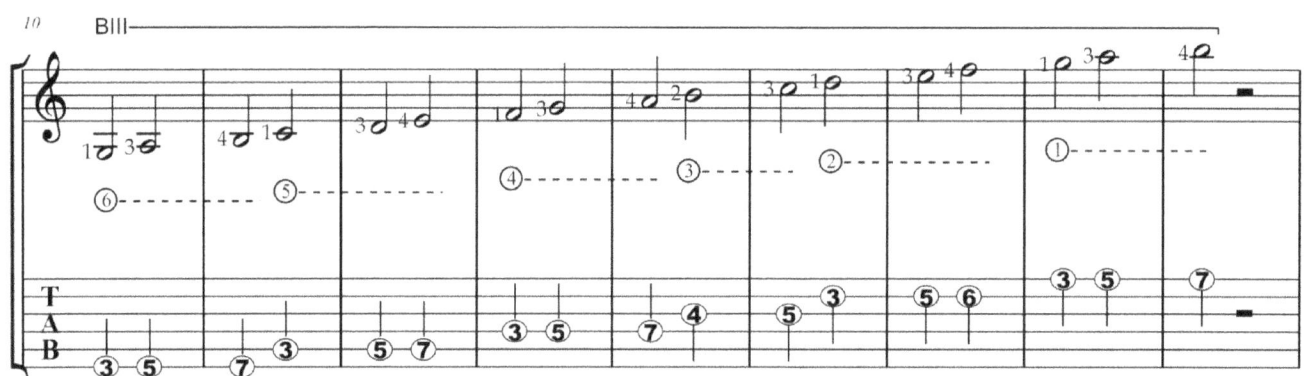
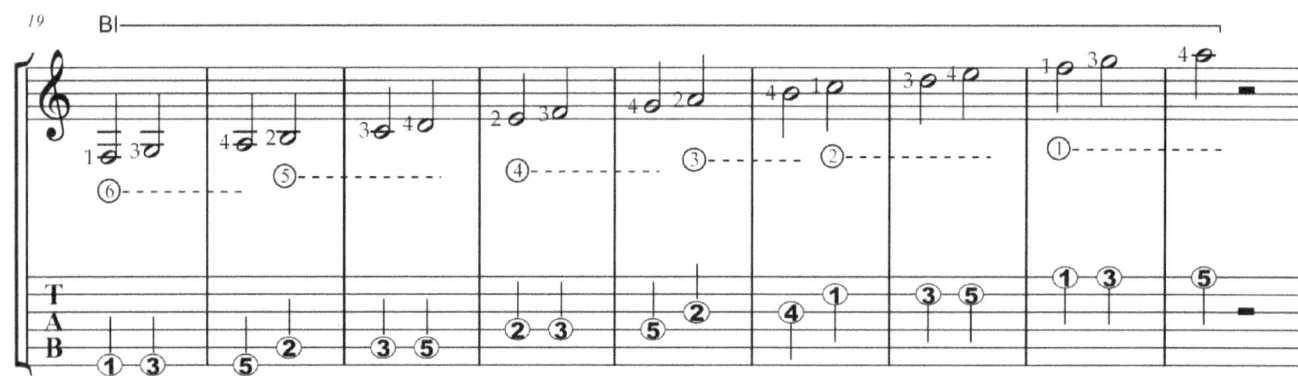

ADVANCED BARRE EXERCISE

Develops the ability in the LEFT HAND to hold multiple notes simultaneously with one finger. Develops the strength and stamina to play Barre Chords and the dexterity to play single note passages featuring barred fingering.

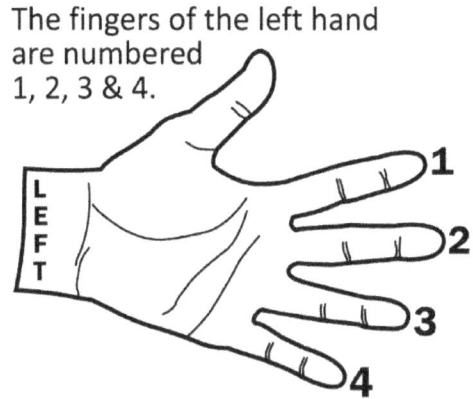

The fingers of the left hand are numbered 1, 2, 3 & 4.

The Advanced Barre Excercise consists of 4 new scale patterns played using a Full Barre with Finger 1 on Fret 1.

Put Finger 1 across all six strings on Fret 1. (full barre)
Play each of the patterns shown below.
DO NOT LIFT FINGER 1 as you play the other notes.

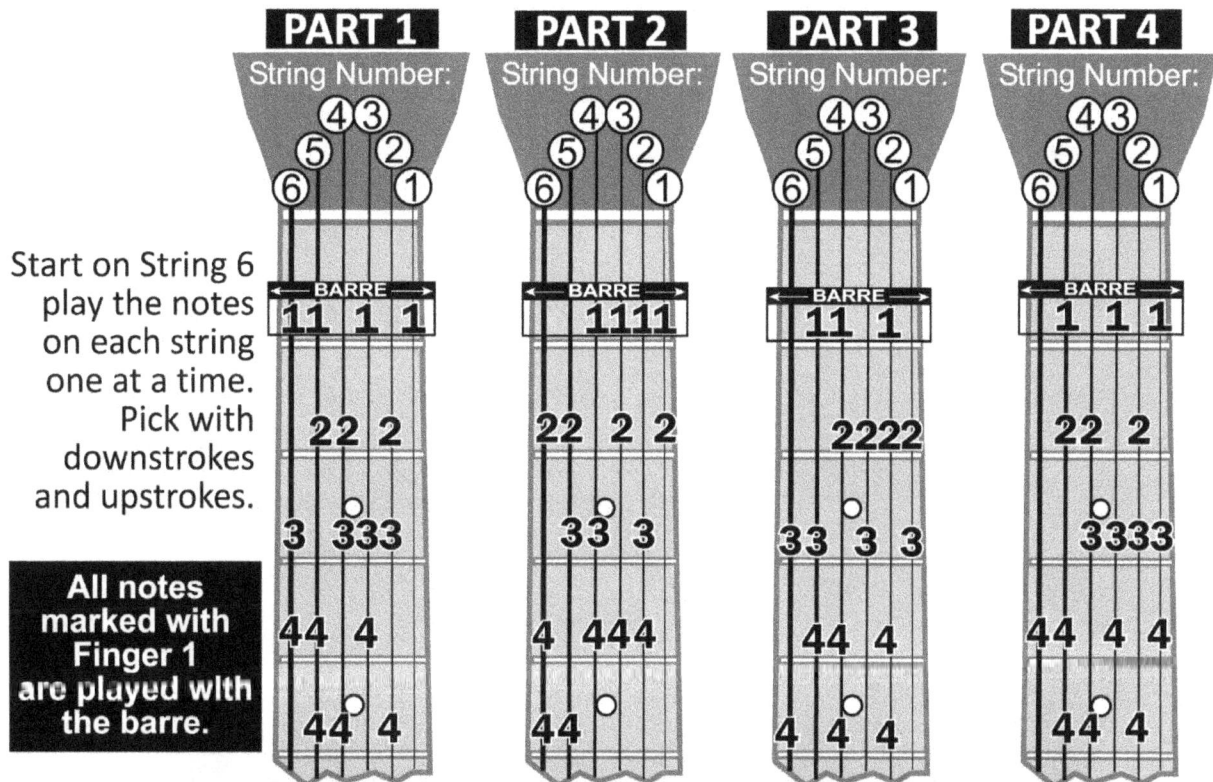

Start on String 6 play the notes on each string one at a time. Pick with downstrokes and upstrokes.

All notes marked with Finger 1 are played with the barre.

Always play this exercise slowly.
Strive to sound the notes played with the bar as cleanly as possible.
Tips on holding a full barre are provided on page 73.

The Advanced Barre Exercise is presented on the following pages in Standard Notation and TAB.

> To hold a barre keep the
> thumb at the back of the neck
> as shown on page 73.

ADVANCED BARRE EXERCISE

Hold the barre on the first fret. All "1" fingerings are played with the barre.

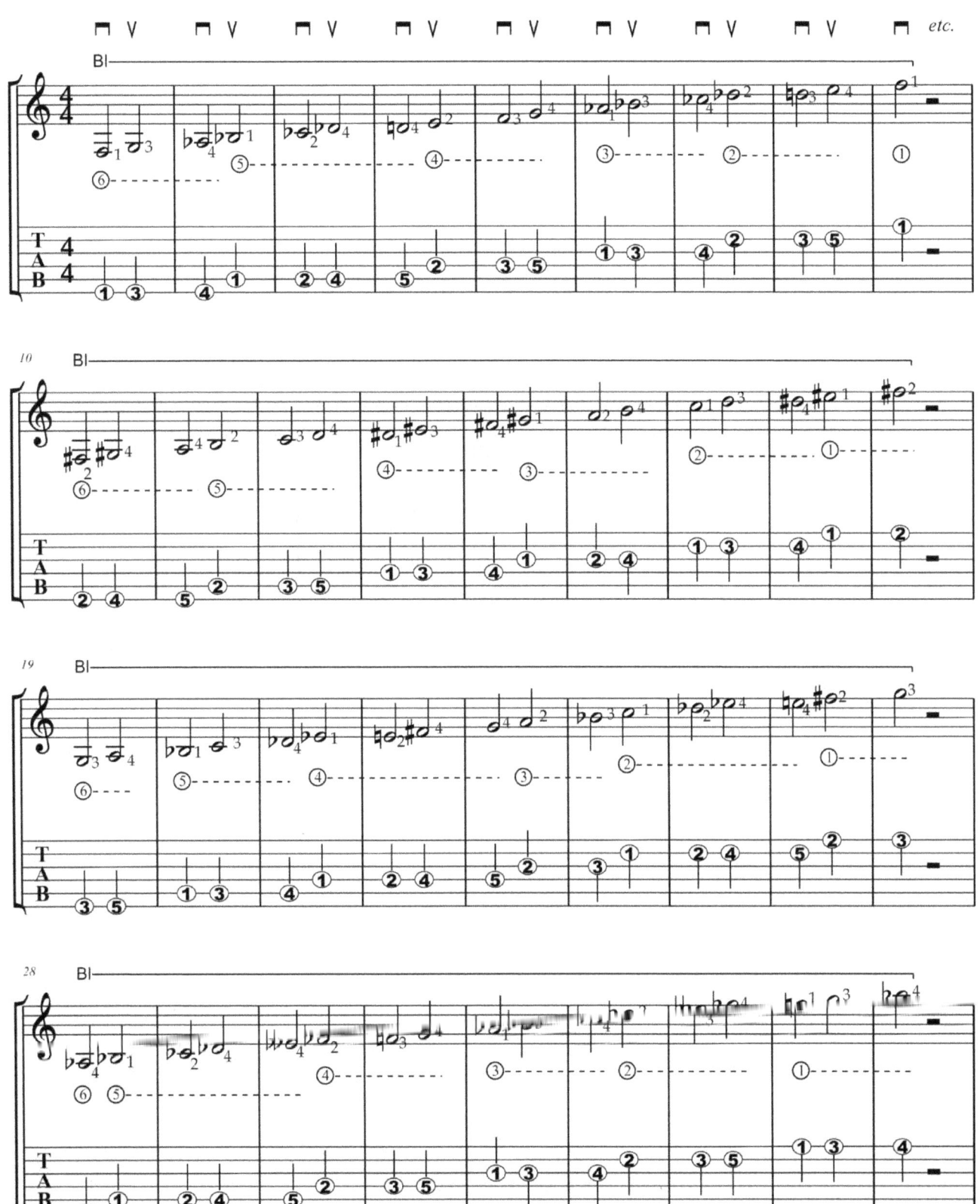

Stretching the left hand is like stretching a rubber band. If you do it slowly and hold a rubber band out it will eventually stretch to that end. The left hand is the same way. If the hand starts to hurt, stop.

9. STRETCH EXERCISE 1

Develops flexibility in the LEFT HAND, especially between Fingers 1 & 2.
Gives the player the ability to comfortably stretch a 5 fret distance.

The fingers of the left hand are numbered 1, 2, 3 & 4.

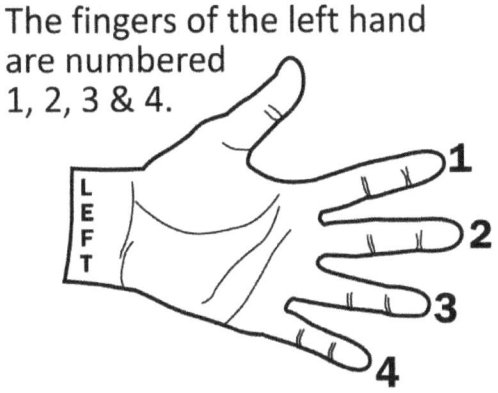

Stretch Exercise 1 is a 5 note sequence played on all 6 Strings.

THIS EXERCISE IS ALWAYS PLAYED VERY SLOWLY.

Start on String 6.

Play a 5 note sequence using these fingers:

1-2-4-2-1

Use this spacing, note the skip over Fret 2 and Fret 4.

Pick with down & up strokes.

LEAVE EACH FINGER ON THE NECK as you play the first 3 notes.

LIFT THE FINGERS one at a time to play the last 2 notes.

REPEAT THE SEQUENCE on **Strings 5, 4, 3, 2 & 1** going across the neck.

REPEAT THE SEQUENCE on **Strings 1, 2, 3, 4, 5 & 6**

END WHERE YOU STARTED.

For optimum results hold the notes down with the finger tips of the left hand. Keep the thumb in the back of the neck. (Refer to the pictures on page 73.)

To achieve an optimum stretch, hold the guitar as recommended on page 71.

Always play this exercise slowly. Performing stretches on the guitar too quickly can cause injury to the hand.

Beginners can pick with all Down Strokes until comfortable.

Stretch Exercise 1 is presented on the following page in Standard Notation and TAB.

STRETCH EXERCISE #1

Very Slowly

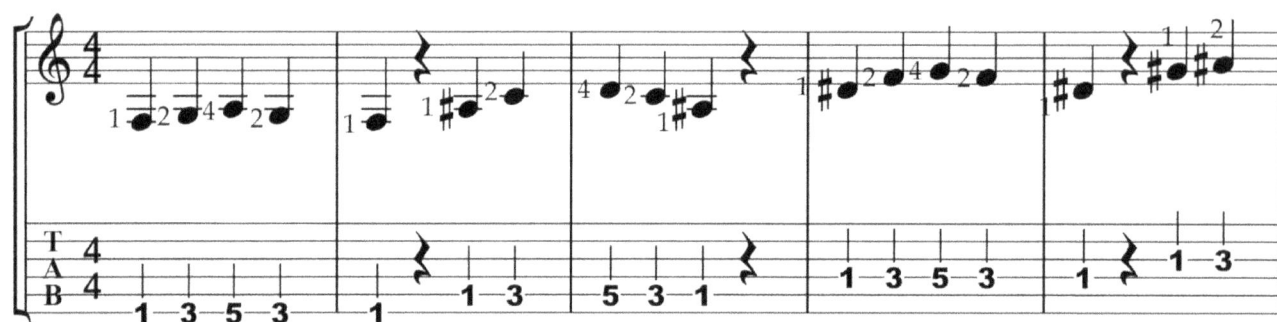
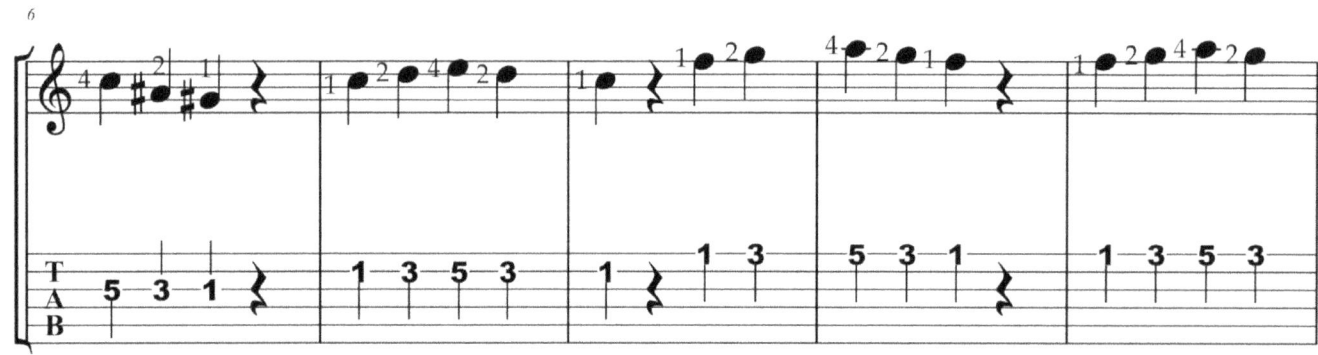

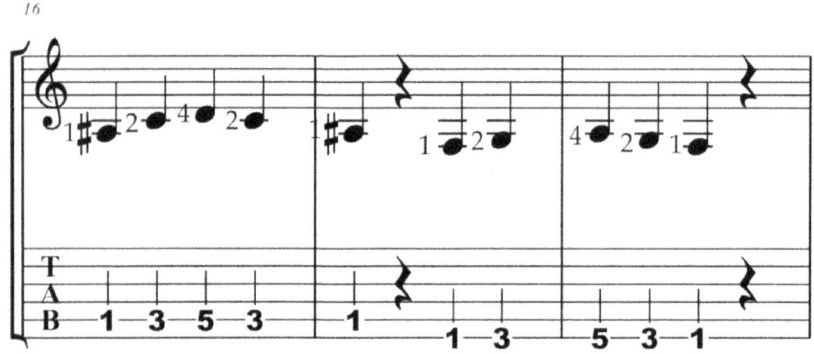

STRETCH EXERCISE 2

*Develops flexibility in the LEFT HAND, especially between Fingers 3 & 4.
Gives the player the ability to comfortably stretch a 5 fret distance.*

The fingers of the left hand are numbered 1, 2, 3 & 4.

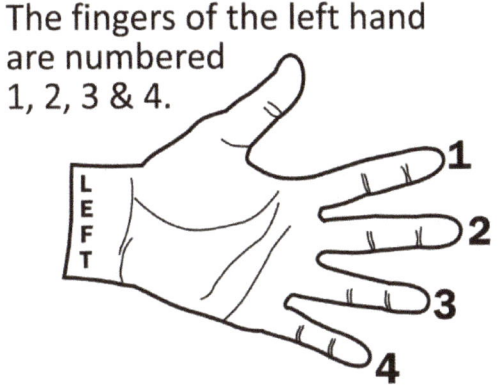

Stretch Exercise 2 uses the same 5 note sequence as Stretch Exercise 1, however this time a different fingering utilized.

THIS EXERCISE IS ALWAYS PLAYED VERY SLOWLY.

Start on String 6.

Play a 5 note sequence using these fingers:

1-3-4-3-1

Use this spacing, note the skip over Fret 2 and Fret 4.

Pick with down & up strokes.

LEAVE EACH FINGER ON THE NECK as you play the first 3 notes.
LIFT THE FINGERS one at a time to play the last 2 notes.

REPEAT THE SEQUENCE on **Strings 5, 4, 3, 2 & 1** going across the neck.

REPEAT THE SEQUENCE on **Strings 1, 2, 3, 4, 5 & 6**

END WHERE YOU STARTED.

For optimum results hold the notes down with the finger tips of the left hand. Keep the thumb in the back of the neck. (Refer to the pictures on page 73.)

To achieve an optimum stretch, hold the guitar as recommended on page 71.

Always play this exercise slowly. Performing stretches on the guitar too quickly can cause injury to the hand.

Beginners can pick with all Down Strokes until comfortable.

Stretch Exercise 2 is presented on the following page in Standard Notation and TAB.

STRETCH EXERCISE #2

Very Slowly

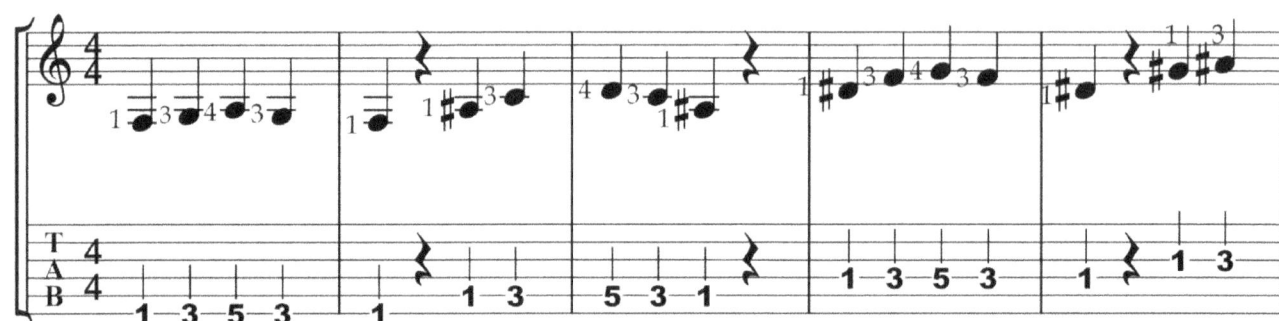
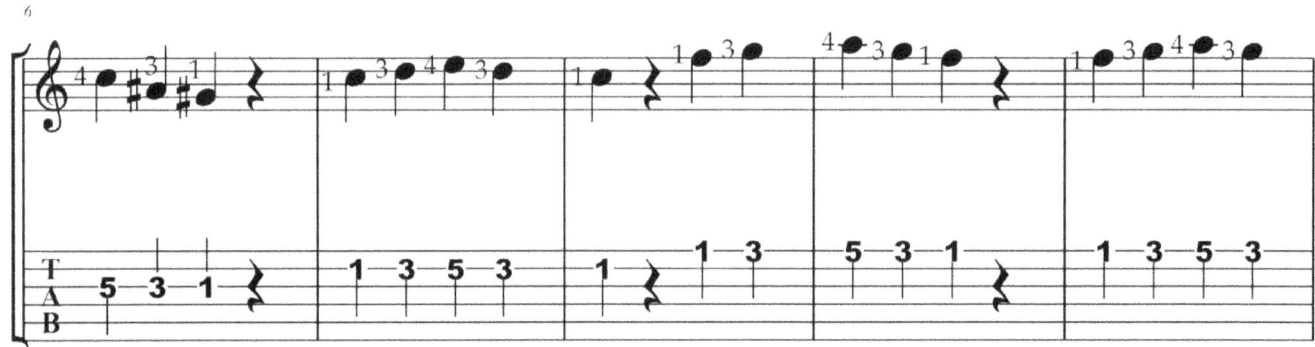

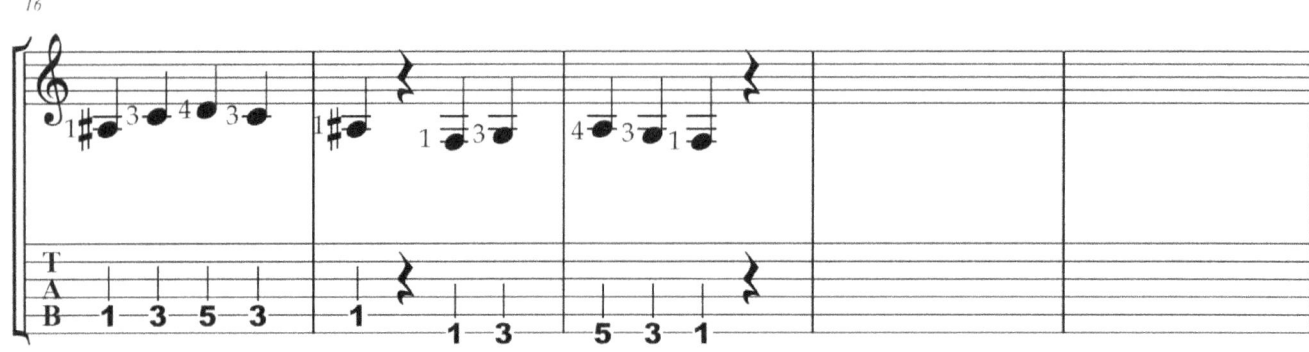

STRETCH EXERCISE 3

Develops flexibility and the ability to stretch a six fret distance with the LEFT HAND.

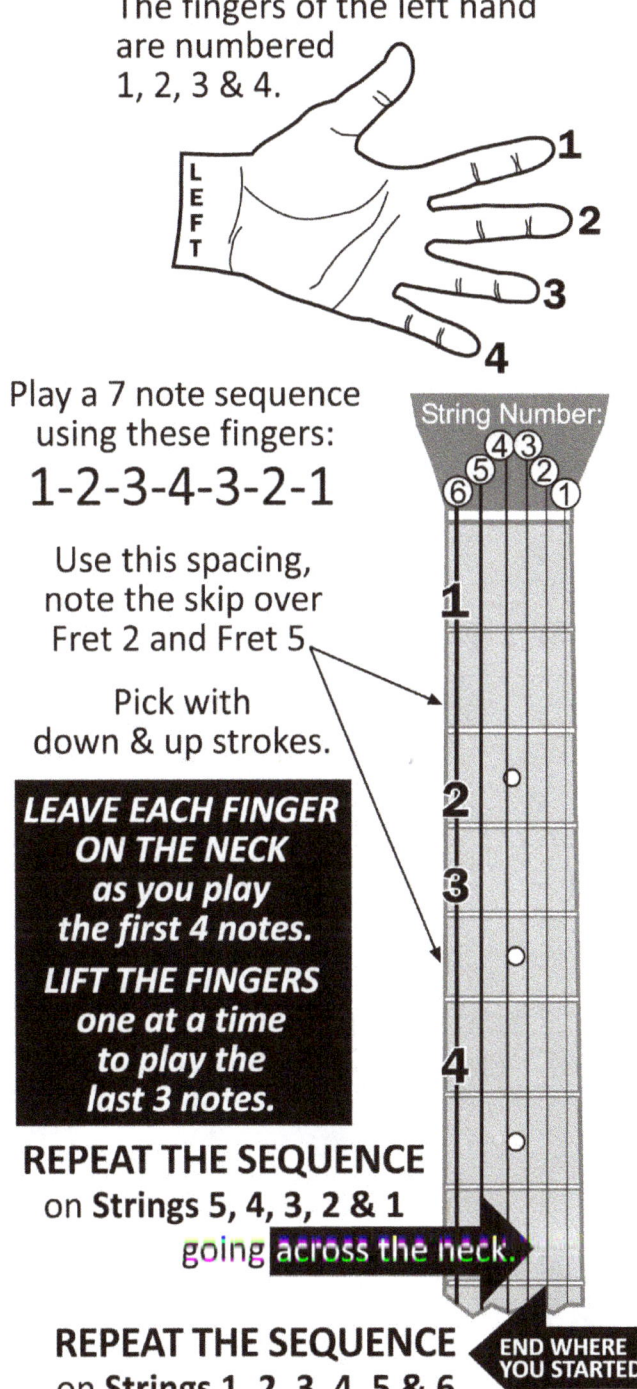

The fingers of the left hand are numbered 1, 2, 3 & 4.

The Stretch Exercise is a 7 note sequence played on all 6 Strings.

THIS EXERCISE IS ALWAYS PLAYED VERY SLOWLY.

Play a 7 note sequence using these fingers:

1-2-3-4-3-2-1

Use this spacing, note the skip over Fret 2 and Fret 5.

Pick with down & up strokes.

LEAVE EACH FINGER ON THE NECK as you play the first 4 notes.

LIFT THE FINGERS one at a time to play the last 3 notes.

REPEAT THE SEQUENCE on **Strings 5, 4, 3, 2 & 1** going across the neck.

For optimum results hold the notes down with the finger tips of the left hand. Keep the thumb in the back of the neck. (Refer to the pictures on page 73.)

To achieve an optimum stretch, hold the guitar as recommended on page 71.

Always play this exercise slowly. Performing stretches on the guitar too quickly can cause injury to the hand.

REPEAT THE SEQUENCE on **Strings 1, 2, 3, 4, 5 & 6**

END WHERE YOU STARTED.

Stretch Exercise 3 is presented on the following pages in Standard Notation and TAB.

41

STRETCH EXERCISE 3

Very Slowly

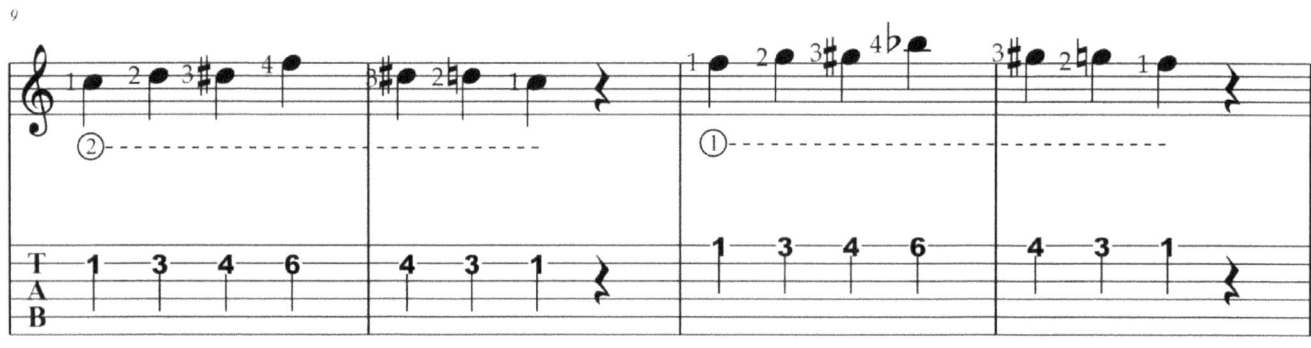
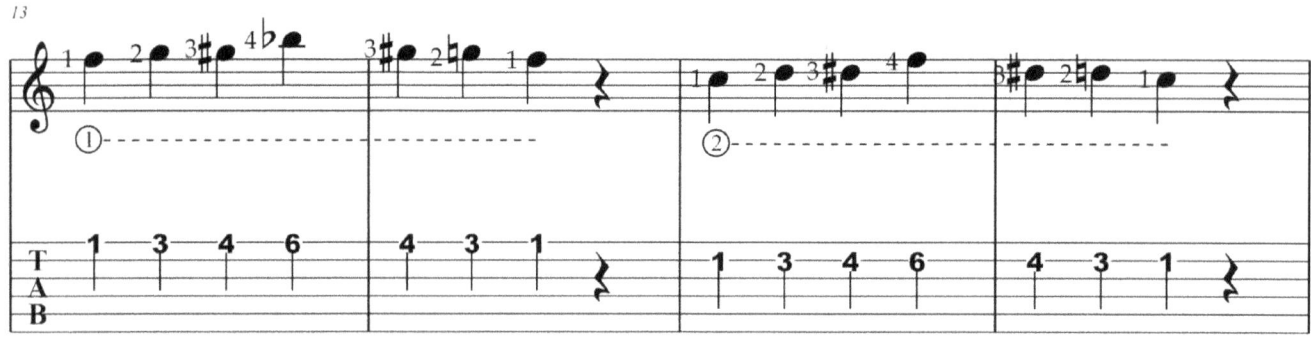

As with the Arpeggio section, the control of the pick on up strokes usually presents a problem doing Double Stops.

Here are 3 suggestions for the right hand on perfecting up strokes:

1. Don't turn the right hand.
2. Don't make broad strokes that cause the right hand to come out or away from the strings.
3. Don't bend the thumb holding the pick.

10. DOUBLE STOPS

The premier exercise to develop dexterity in ALL FINGERS of the LEFT HAND. Fosters accurate multiple string picking with the RIGHT HAND.

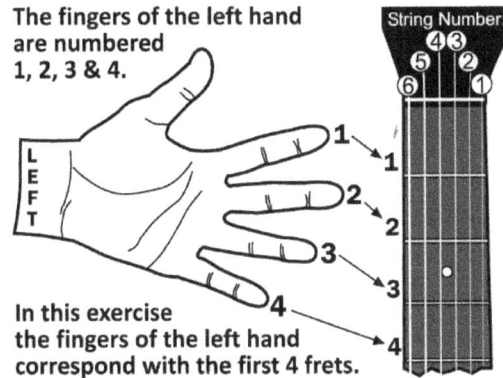

The fingers of the left hand are numbered 1, 2, 3 & 4.

In this exercise the fingers of the left hand correspond with the first 4 frets.

Double Stops are 12 sets of intervals played in pairs. The full exercise is repeated 6 times, using different picking patterns.

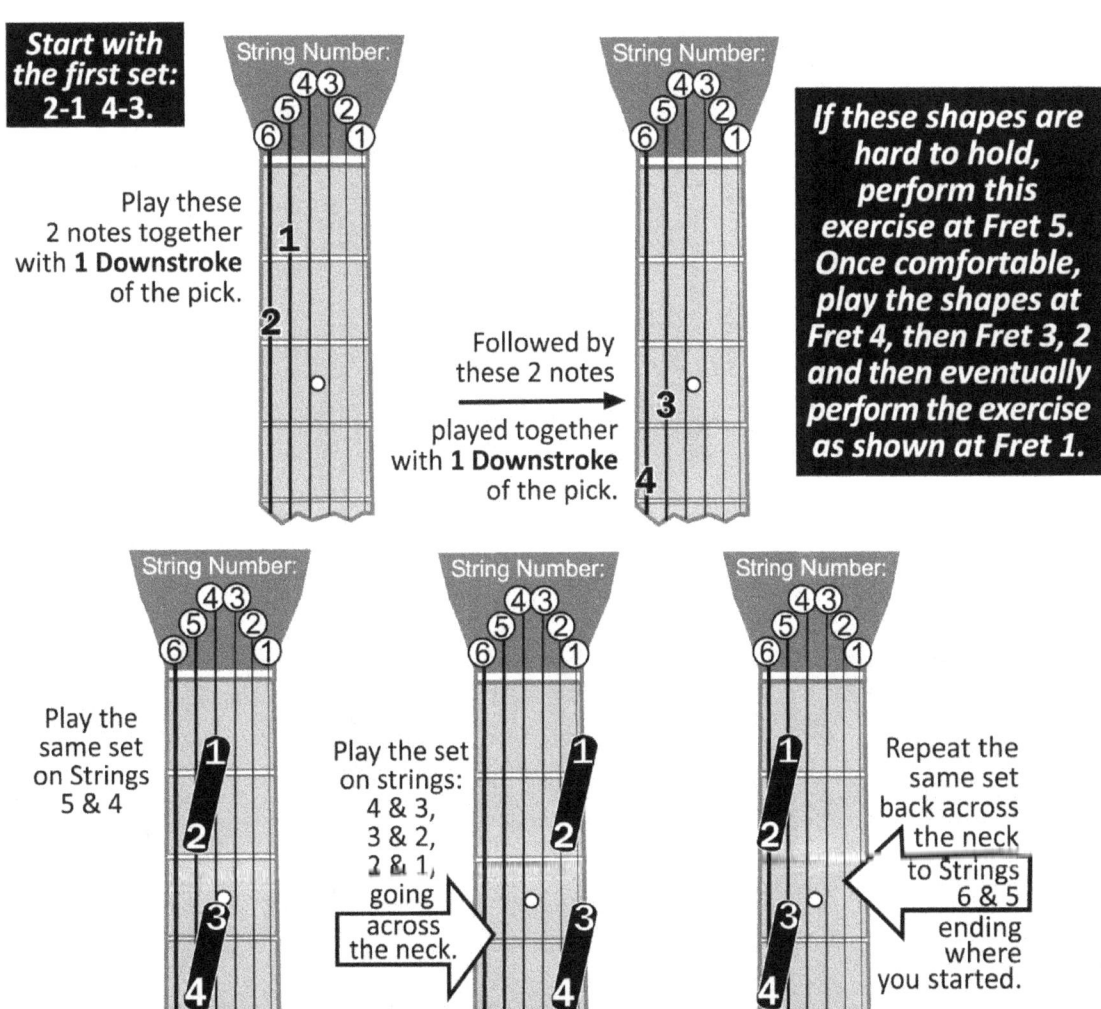

Start with the first set: 2-1 4-3.

Play these 2 notes together with **1 Downstroke** of the pick.

Followed by these 2 notes played together with **1 Downstroke** of the pick.

If these shapes are hard to hold, perform this exercise at Fret 5. Once comfortable, play the shapes at Fret 4, then Fret 3, 2 and then eventually perform the exercise as shown at Fret 1.

Play the same set on Strings 5 & 4

Play the set on strings: 4 & 3, 3 & 2, 2 & 1, going across the neck.

Repeat the same set back across the neck to Strings 6 & 5 ending where you started.

Play the remaining 11 sets shown on the next page on all strings as described above:

Play the following 11 sets on all strings as described on the previous page.

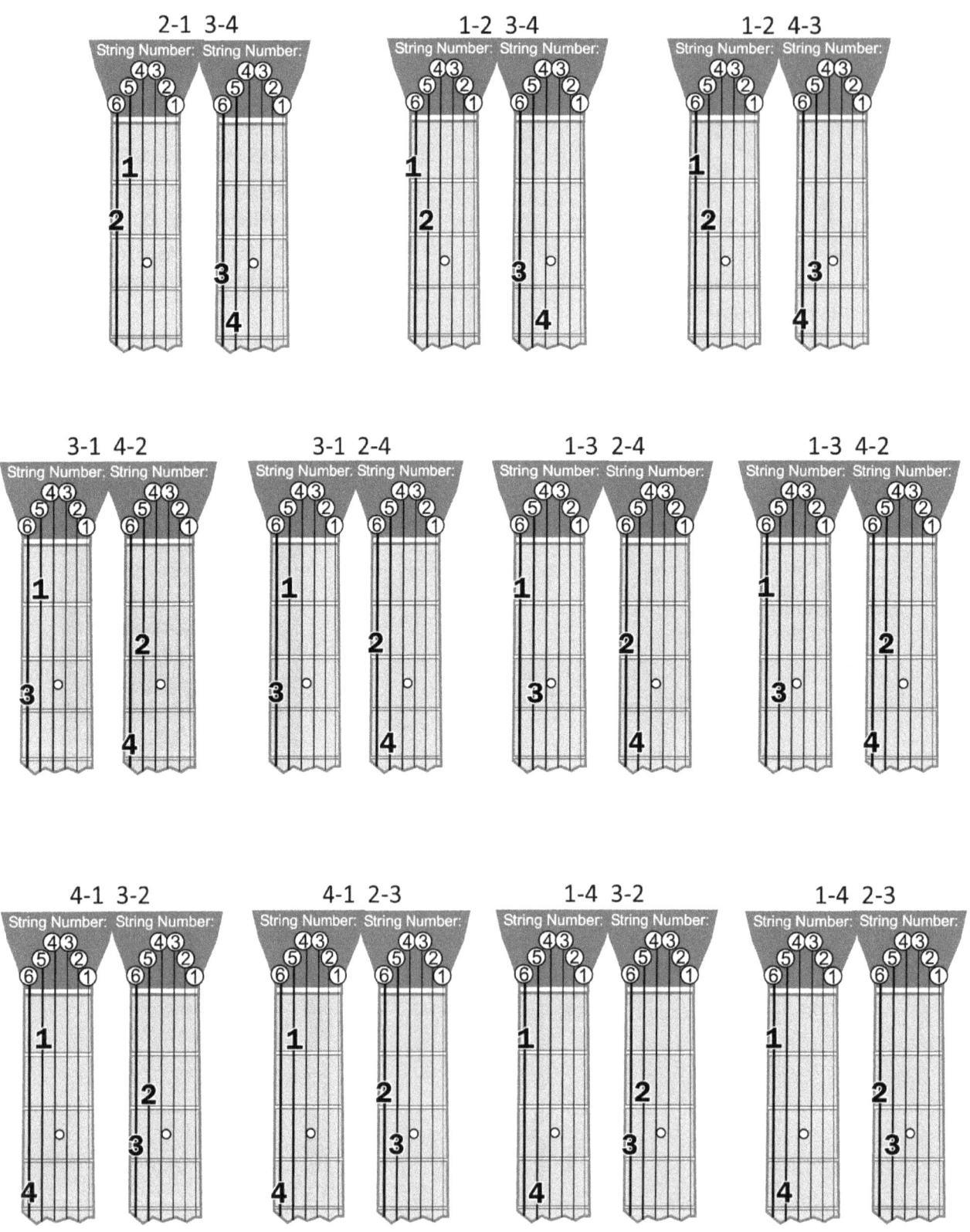

Perform this exercise at Fret 5 if you have trouble holding these shapes at Fret 1.

Now repeat the 12 sets using picking patterns 2, 3 & 4:

1. (⊓⊓) Pick both notes of each interval with 1 Downstroke.
2. (V V) Pick both notes of each interval with 1 Upstroke.
3. (⊓ V) Pick both notes of Interval 1 with a Downstroke
   & pick both notes of Interval 2 with an Upstroke.
4. (V ⊓) Pick both notes of Interval 1 with an Upstroke
   & pick both notes of Interval 2 with a Downstroke.

Now play the 12 sets as single notes*:

5. (⊓ V ⊓ V) Pick the first note of Interval 1 with a Downstroke
   & the second note of Interval 1 with an Upstroke.
   Pick Interval 2 the same way.
6. (V ⊓ V ⊓) Pick the first note of Interval 1 with an Upstroke &
   the second note of Interval 1 with a Downstroke.
   Pick Interval 2 the same way.

*Though the notes are picked as single notes continue putting both fingers of each interval on the neck at the same time.

Double Stops are presented on the following pages in Standard Notation and TAB.

DOUBLE STOPS

DOUBLE STOPS
(Continued)

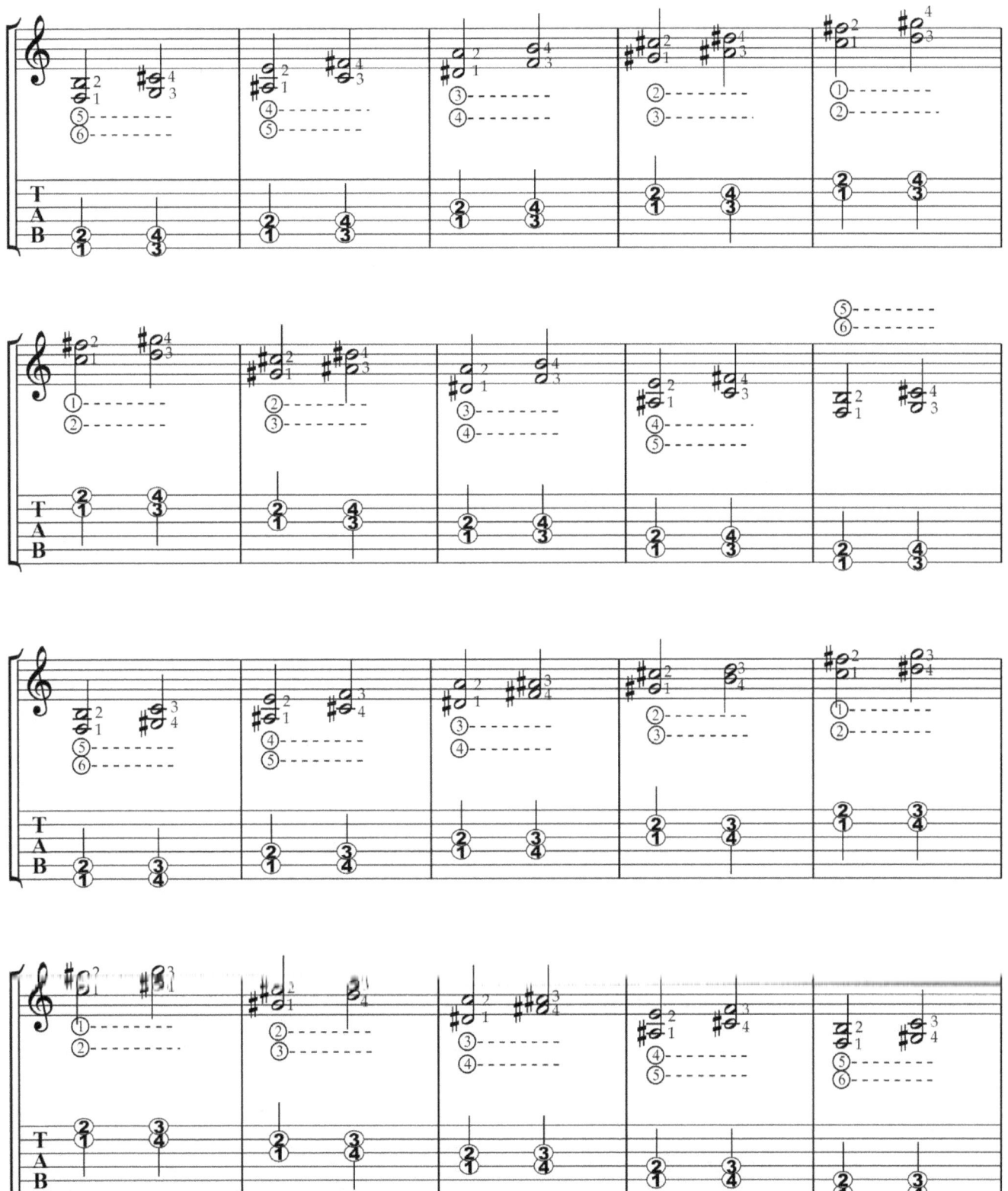

DOUBLE STOPS
(Continued)

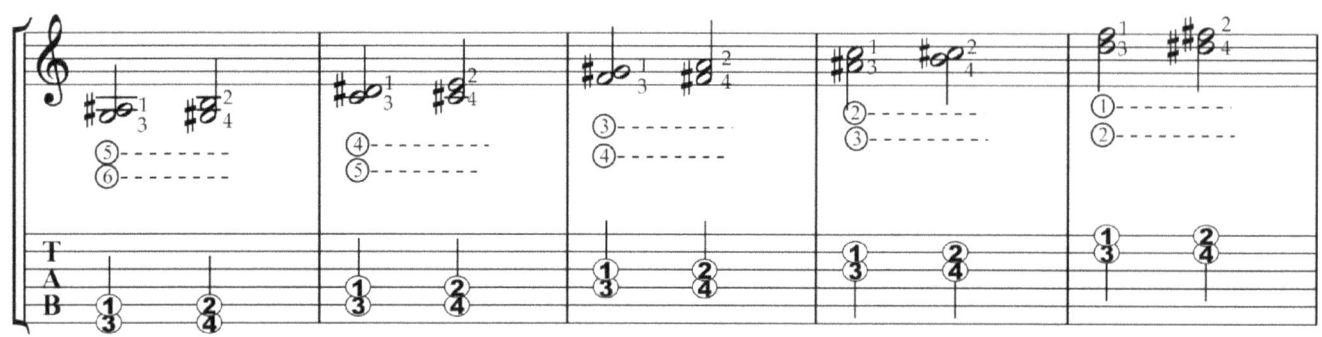
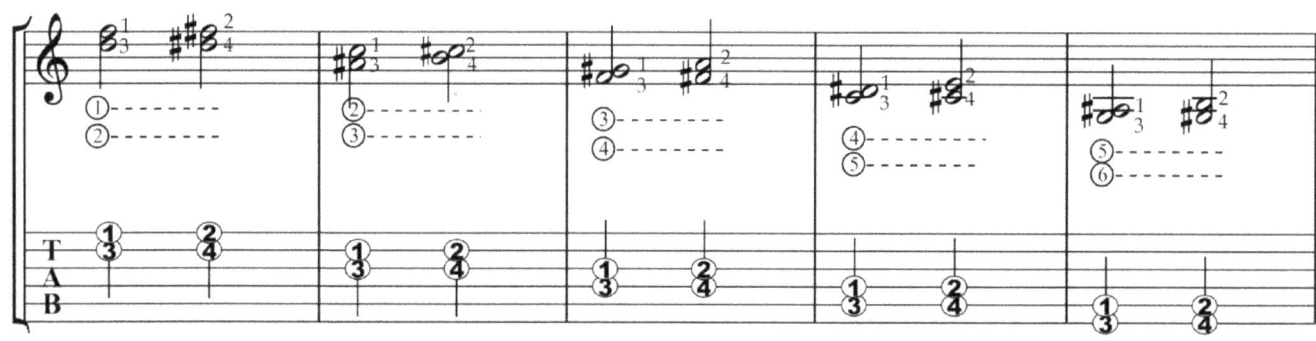
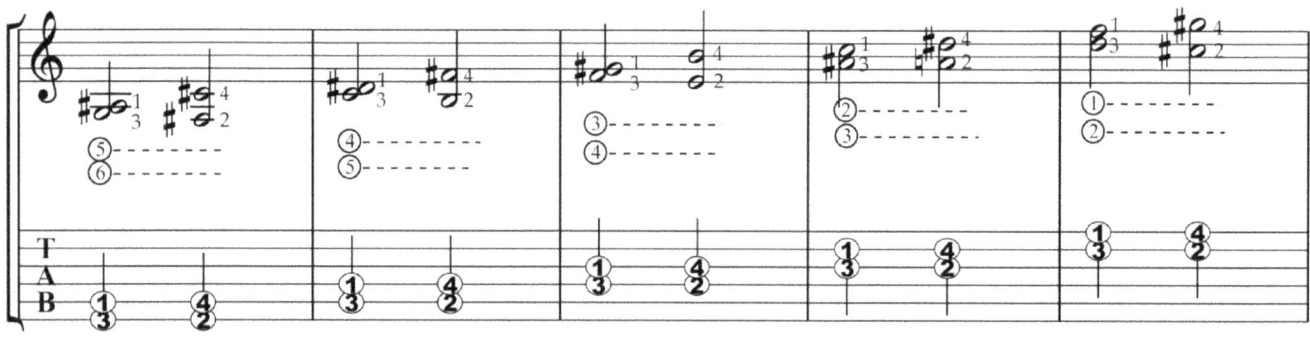
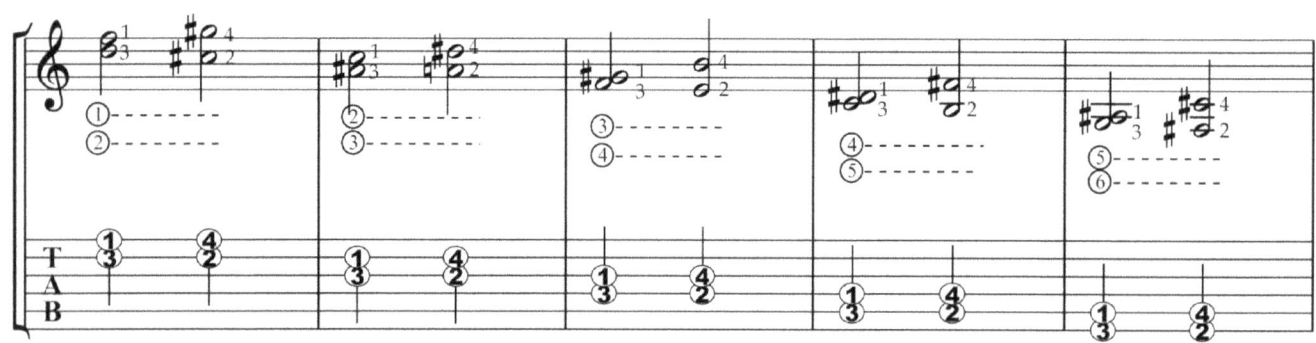

DOUBLE STOPS
(Continued)

DOUBLE STOPS
(Continued)

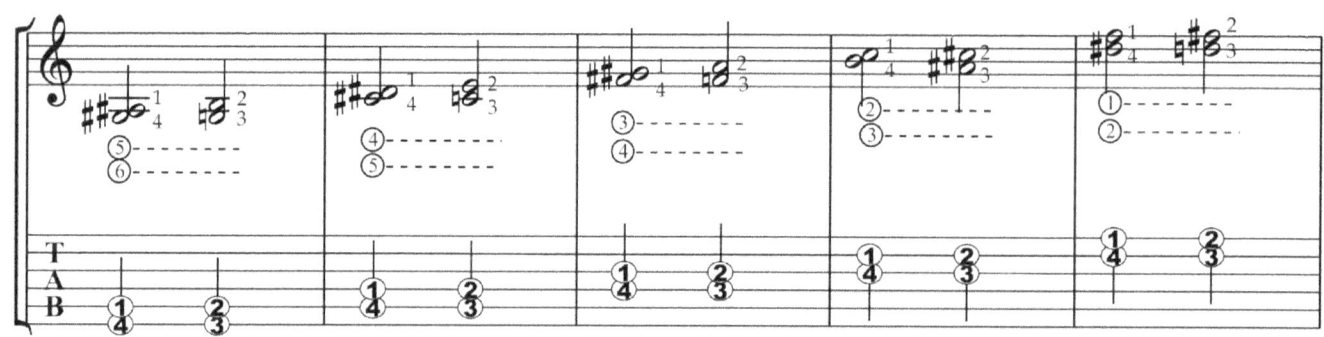
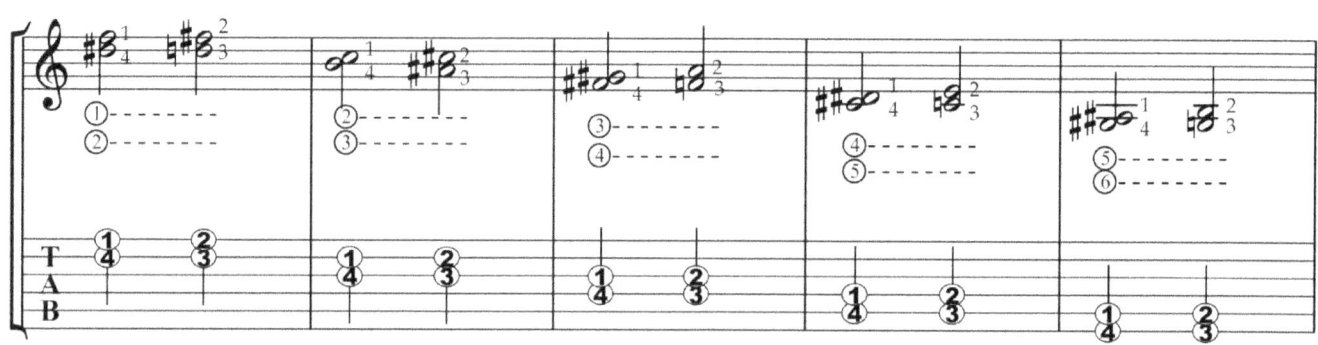
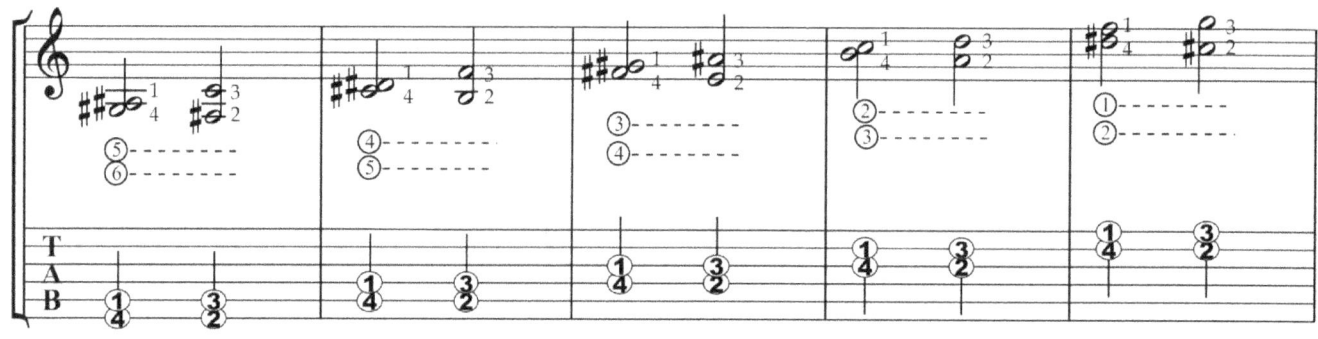
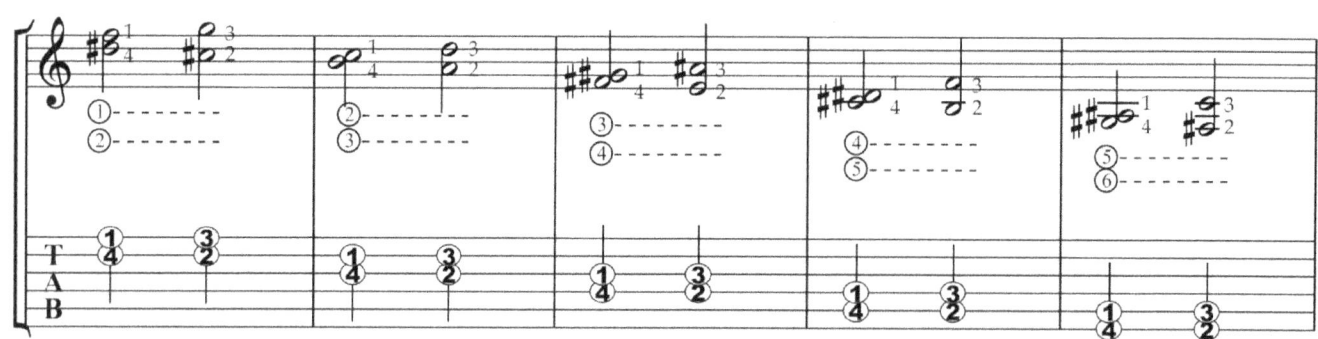

DOUBLE STOPS
(Continued)

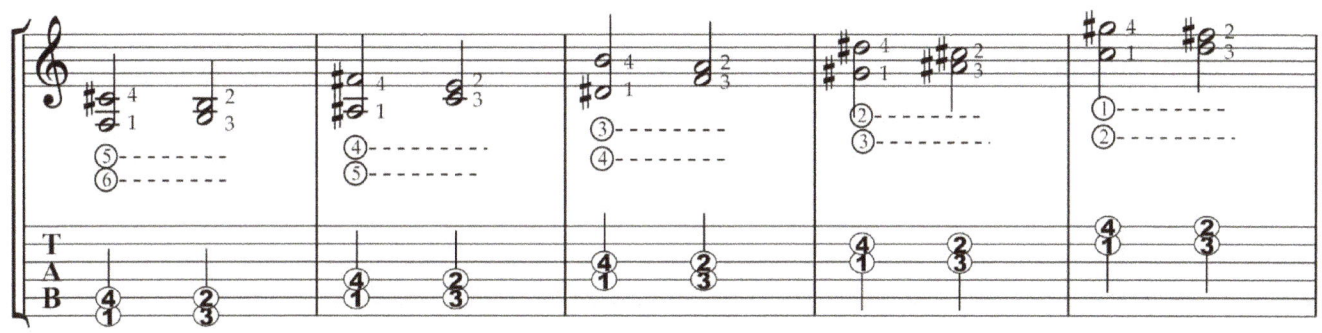
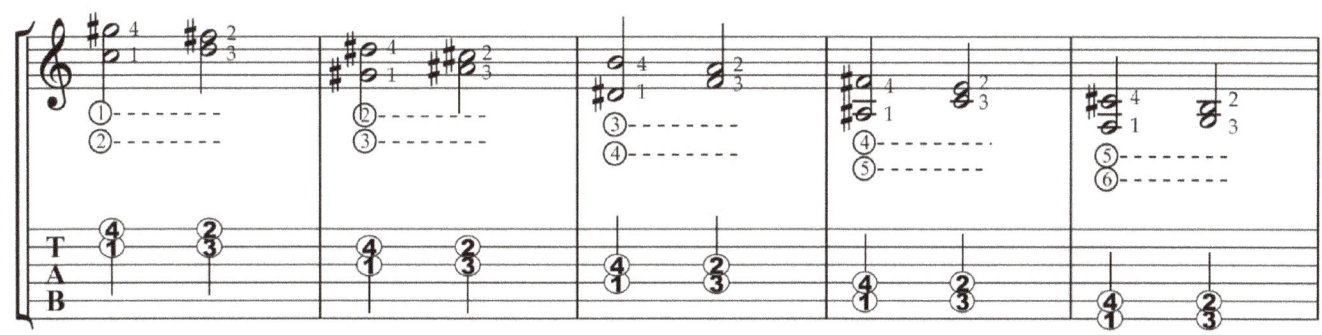
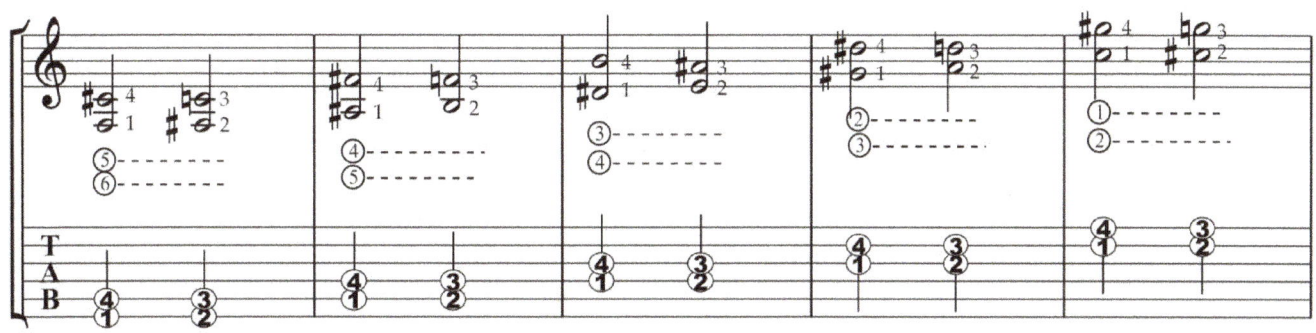
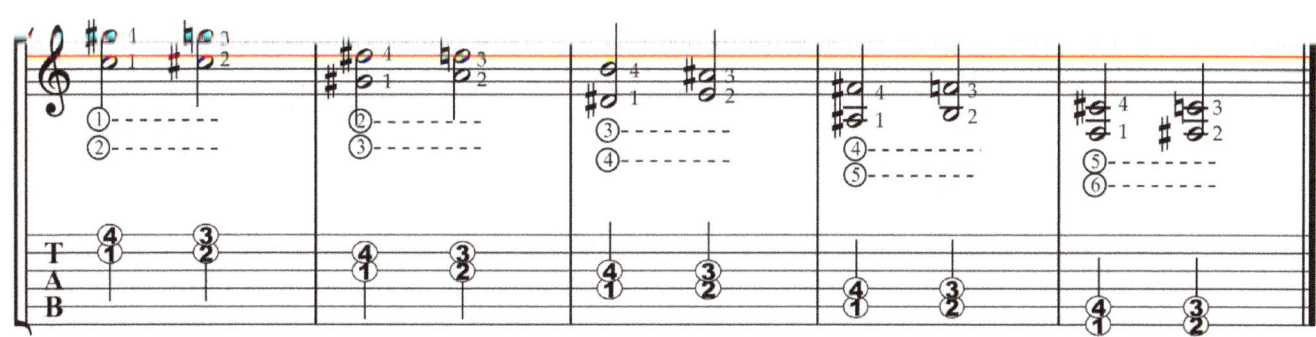

SINGLE NOTE DOUBLE STOPS

*Hold each interval down as before, with both fingers together,
but in these sections pick the notes separately.*

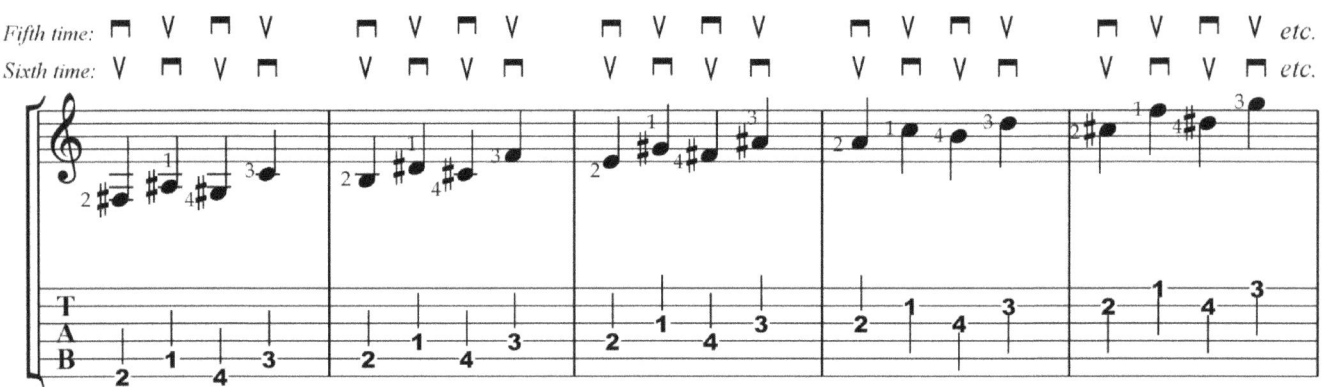

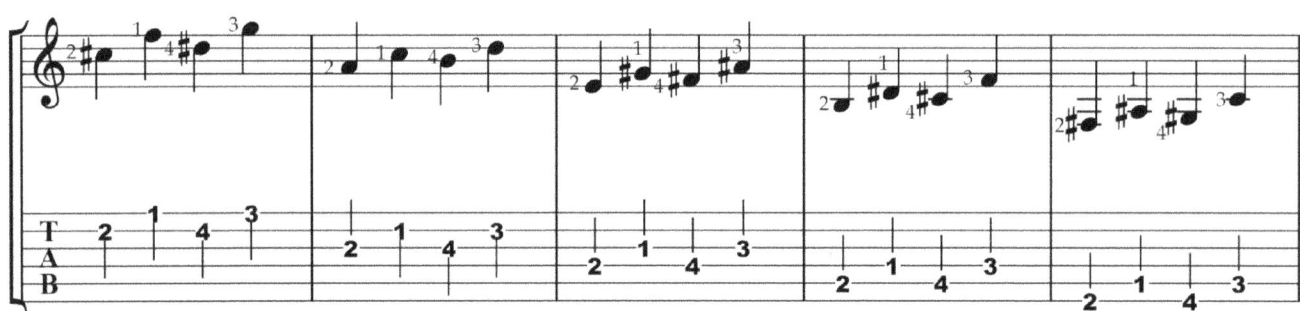

*Play all 12 sets as single notes with Down-Up picking.
Repeat the 12 sets as single notes with Up-Down picking.*

11. DOUBLE STOP SCALES

*Builds on the dexterity acquired in Section 6 (Crosspicking) &
Section 10 (Double Stops). Allows to the ear to recognize harmonic possibilities
when playing 2 notes together.*

The fingers of the left hand are numbered 1, 2, 3 & 4.

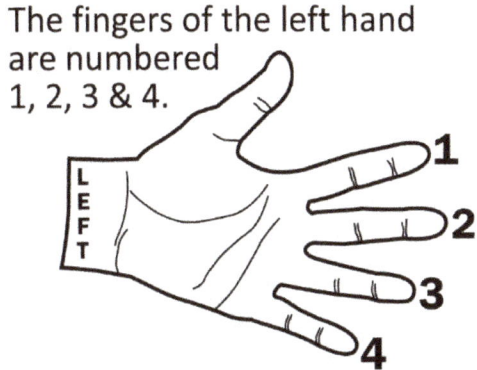

This exercise features new Double Stops using the notes of the C Major Scale.

**The exercise is presented in 2 parts:
Double Stops in 5ths &
Double Stops in 6ths.
Both parts are played
in 5 positions on the neck.**

The first section of Part 1 is presented below in picture diagrams.

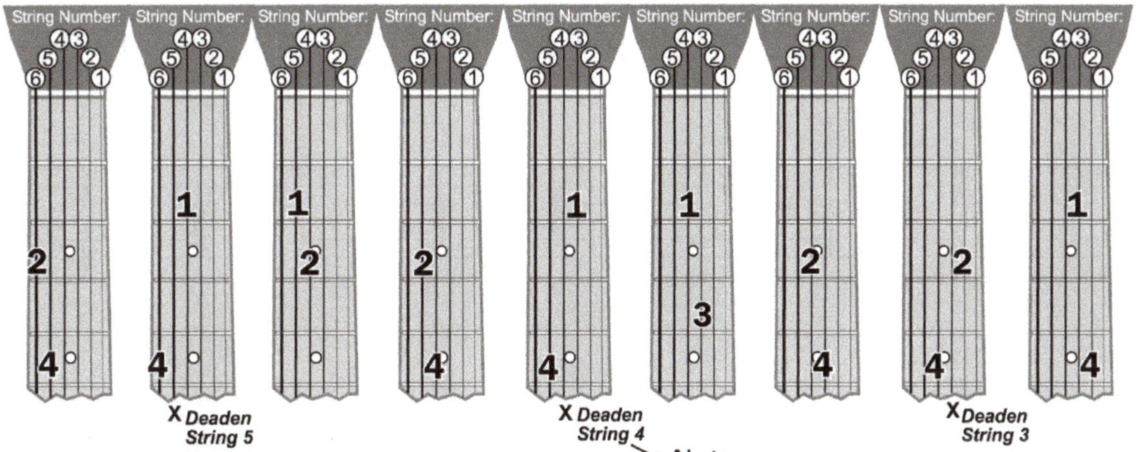

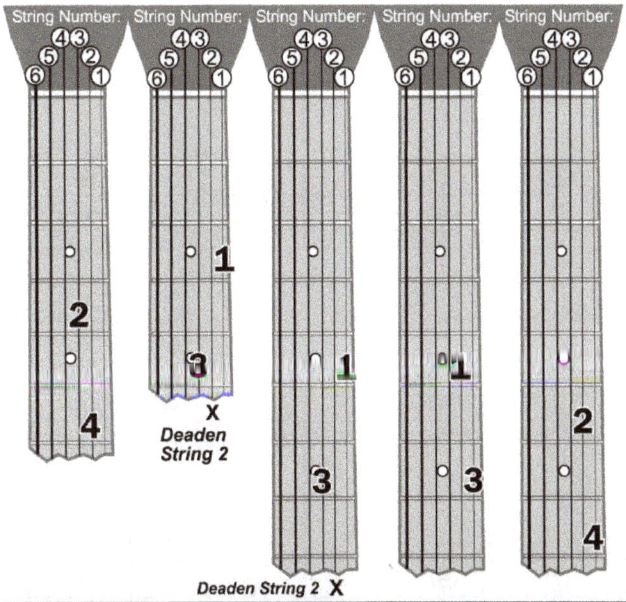

Note...
In this exercise some of the Double Stops are not on adjacent strings.

In these cases you must "**deaden**" the string in between.

(Lightly touch the middle string with an adjacent finger to silence, or deaden, the string.)

Deadening will let you strum right over the string without hearing it.

Players are encouraged at this point to learn the rest of this exercise using the Standard Notation or TAB provided. Tips for reading this material can be found on pages 67, 68, and 69.

Double Stop Scales are presented on the following pages in Standard Notation and TAB.

55

DOUBLE STOPS IN FIFTHS
("C" Scale notes)

Position 7

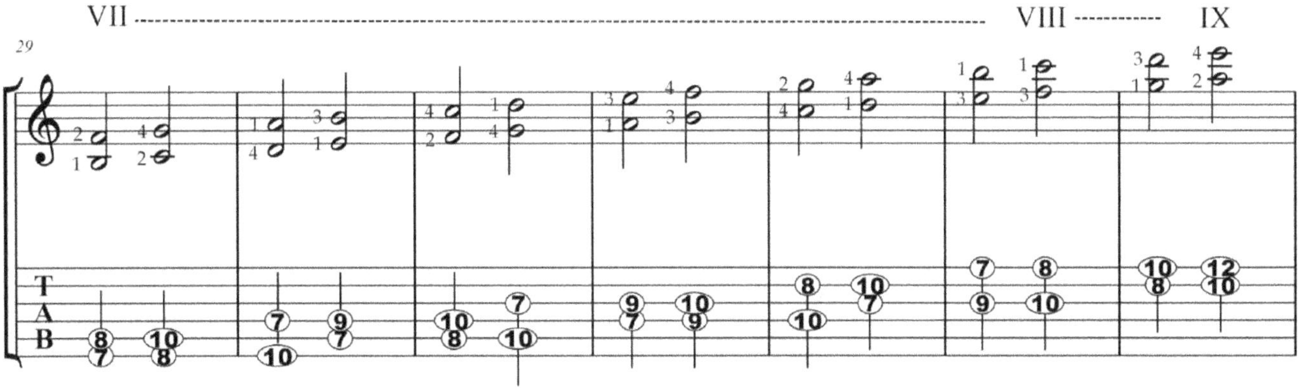

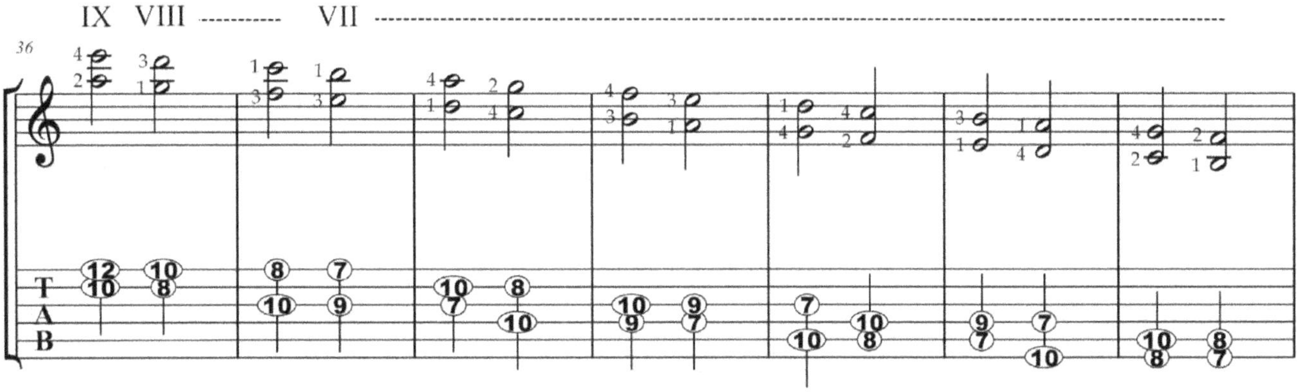

Position 10

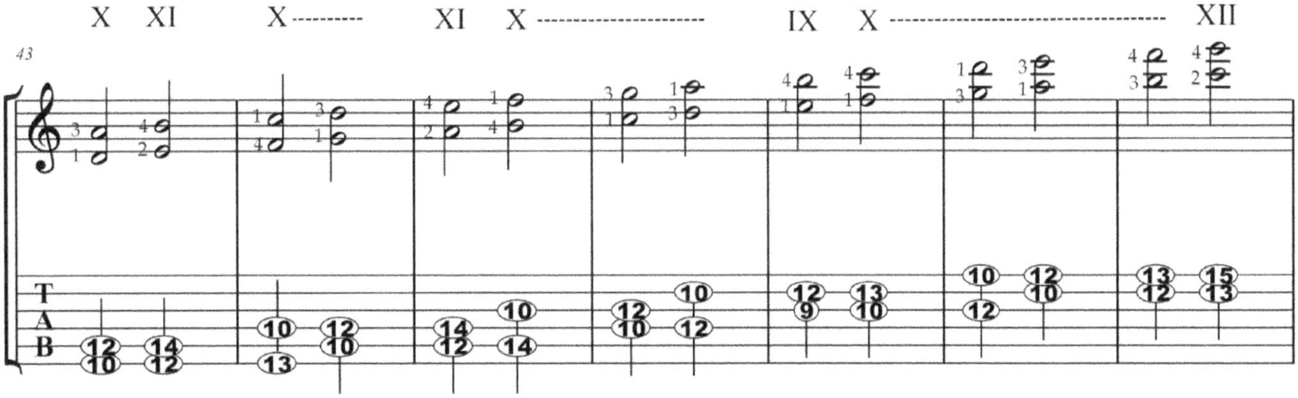

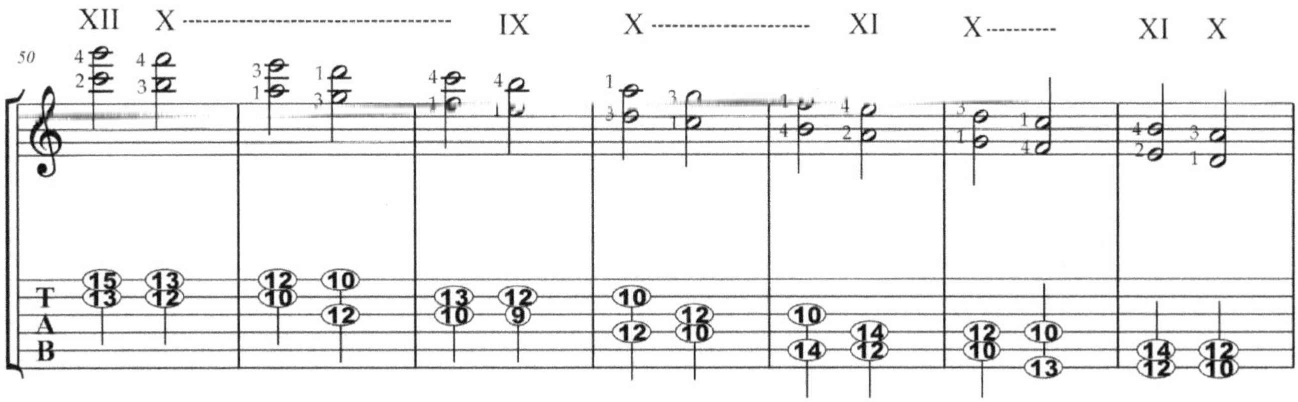

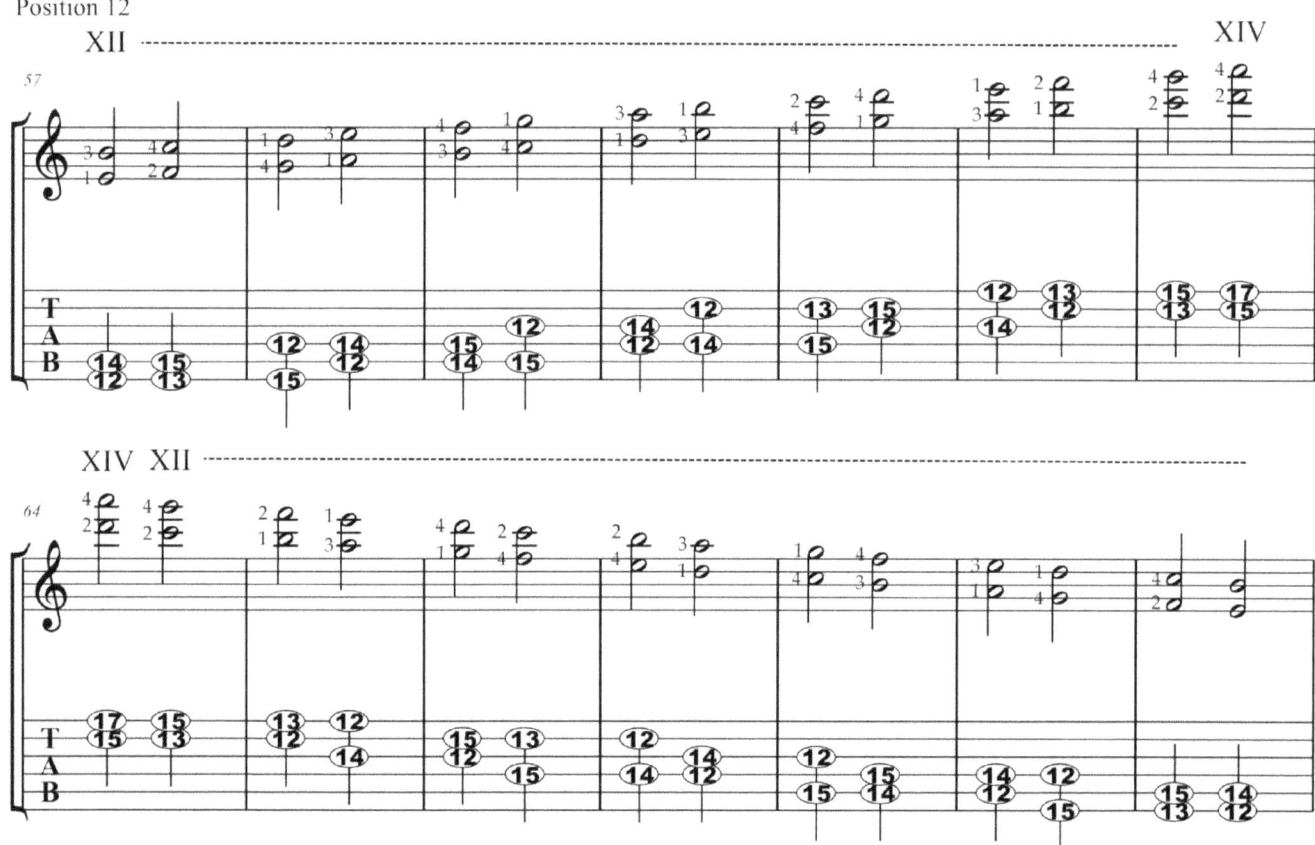

DOUBLE STOPS IN SIXTHS
("C" Scale notes)

Position 7

Position 10

60

Position 12

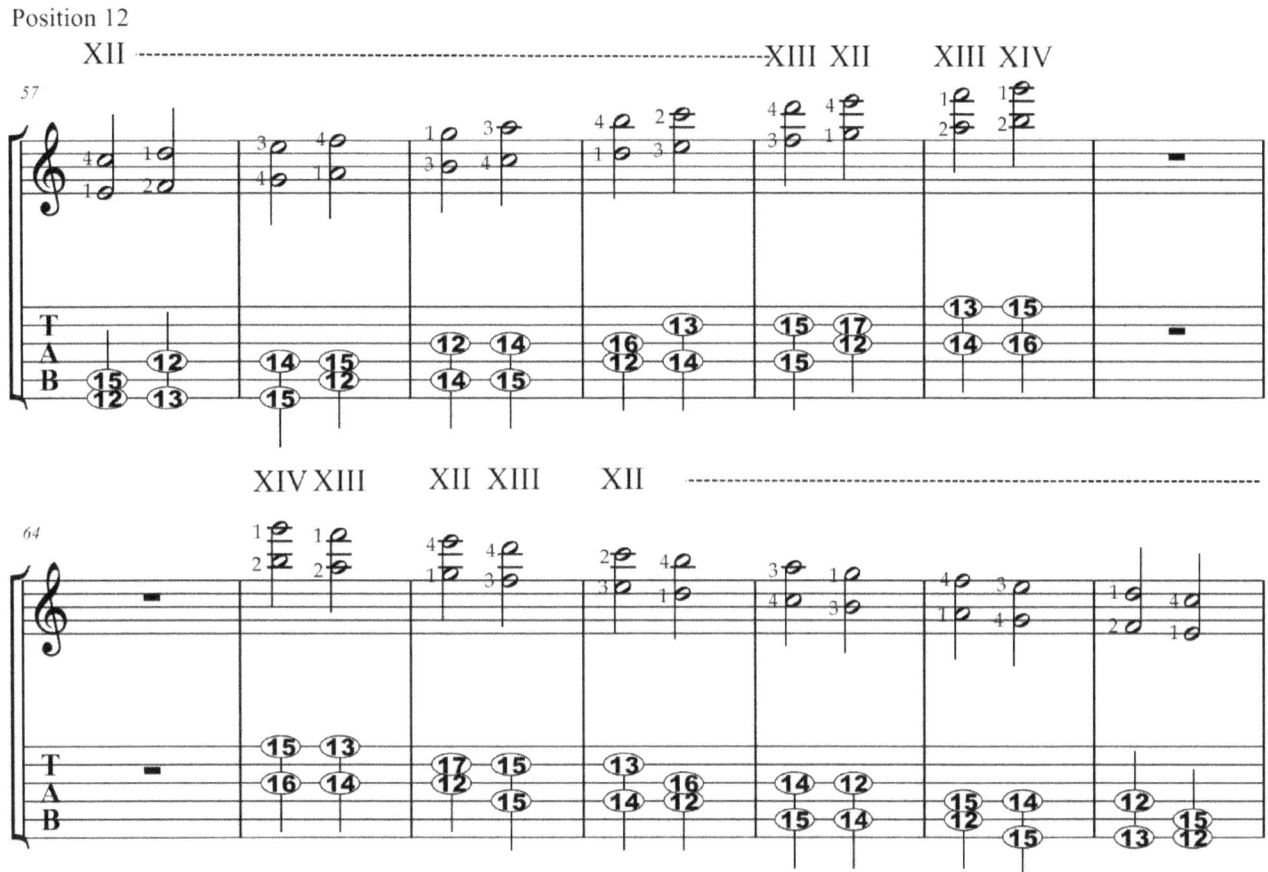

61

> Practicing and playing music where these techniques can be applied will assist the player to broaden his/her horizon as a performer.

12. CHORD SCALE

Develops flexibility and dexterity in the LEFT HAND.
Fosters accurate strumming in the RIGHT HAND.
Allows to the ear to recognize harmonic possibilities in major scales.

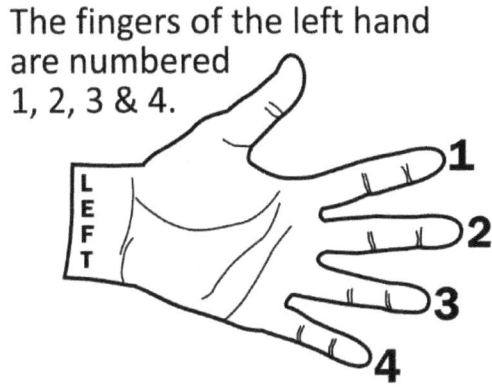

The fingers of the left hand are numbered 1, 2, 3 & 4.

The Chord Scale exercise consists of a C major scale played with chords rather than single notes.

The scale is played 5 times on 5 different string groups. The whole exercise is repeated using a second picking style.

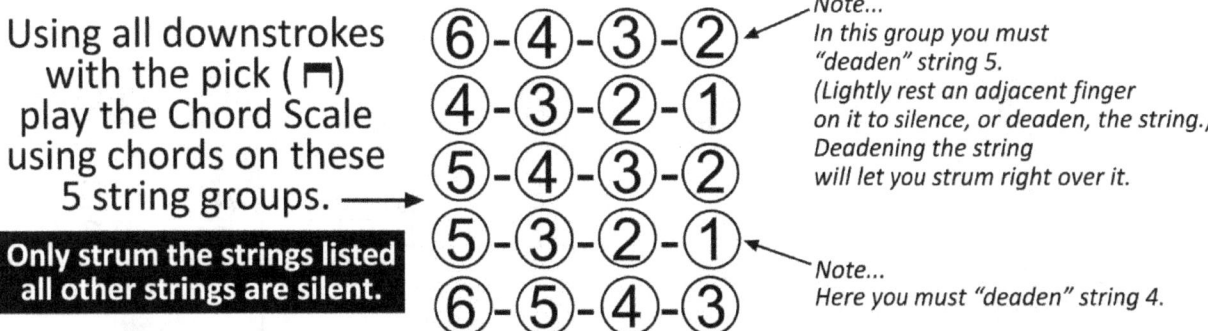

Using all downstrokes with the pick (⊓) play the Chord Scale using chords on these 5 string groups.

⑥-④-③-②
④-③-②-①
⑤-④-③-②
⑤-③-②-①
⑥-⑤-④-③

Note...
In this group you must "deaden" string 5.
(Lightly rest an adjacent finger on it to silence, or deaden, the string.) Deadening the string will let you strum right over it.

Note...
Here you must "deaden" string 4.

Only strum the strings listed all other strings are silent.

Repeat the 5 Chord Scales strumming with Down - Up Strokes (⊓ V)

The 5 Chord Scales are presented as Chord Charts in the standard guitar notation on the following pages.

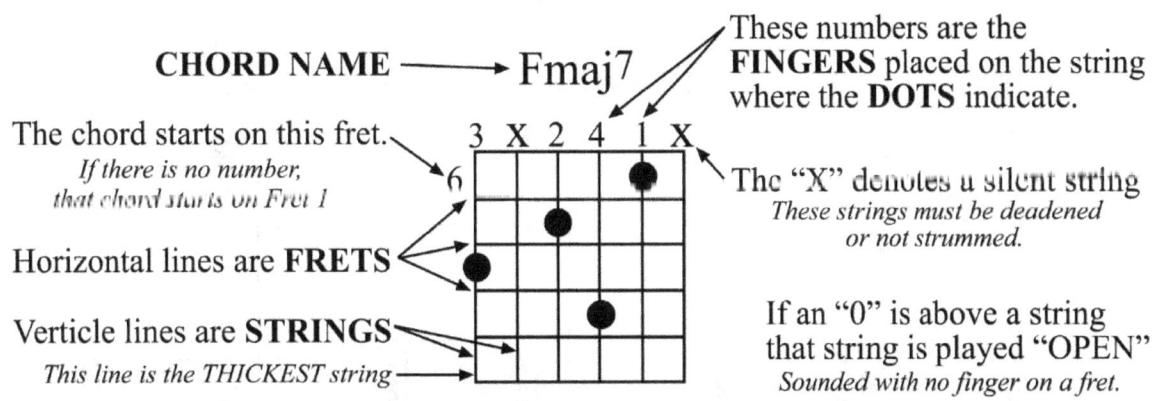

CHORD NAME → Fmaj7

These numbers are the **FINGERS** placed on the string where the **DOTS** indicate.

The chord starts on this fret.
If there is no number, that chord starts on Fret 1

The "X" denotes a silent string
These strings must be deadened or not strummed.

Horizontal lines are **FRETS**

Verticle lines are **STRINGS**
This line is the THICKEST string

If an "0" is above a string that string is played "OPEN"
Sounded with no finger on a fret.

The Chord Scale Exercise is presented on the following pages in Standard Notation and TAB.

CHORD SCALE

These Chord Scales can also be played with the picking styles described in Section 4 (Backpicking) and Section 5 (Alternate Picking).

> This section, though originally intended for beginners, can be helpful to all players, especially those having difficulty mastering the 12 Exercises.

13. FOR BEGINNERS

A BRIEF EXPLANATION OF TAB

Tablature (TAB) is musical notation developed originally for rock guitar, as an addition to standard music notation. Though there are many symbols in TAB, below is an explanation of the TAB shown in this book.

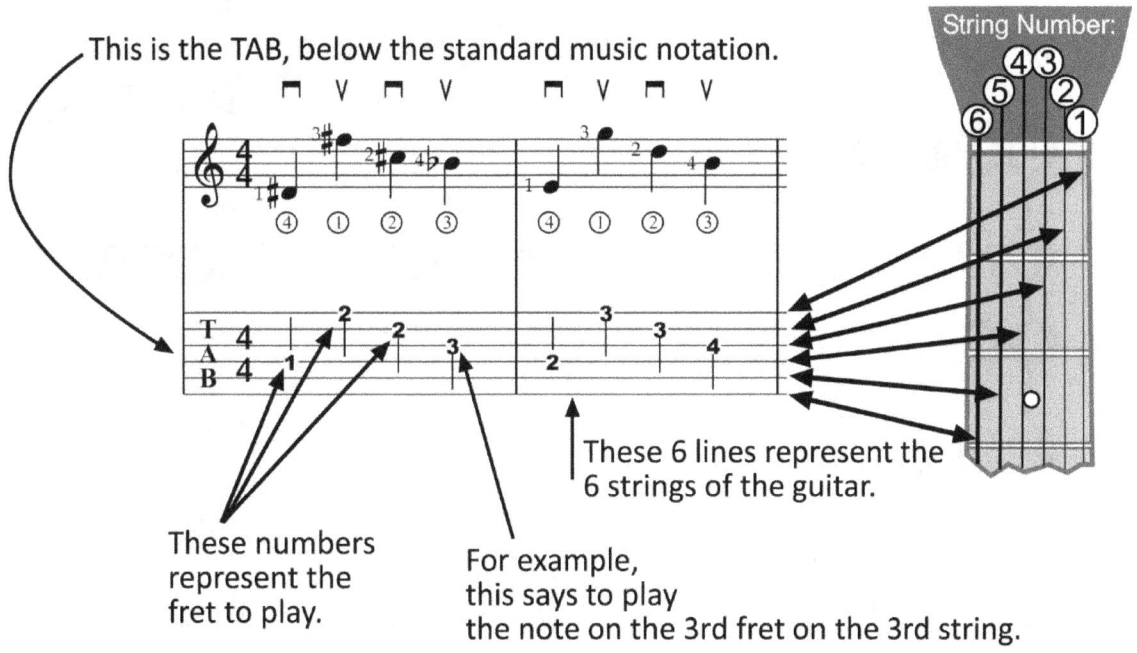

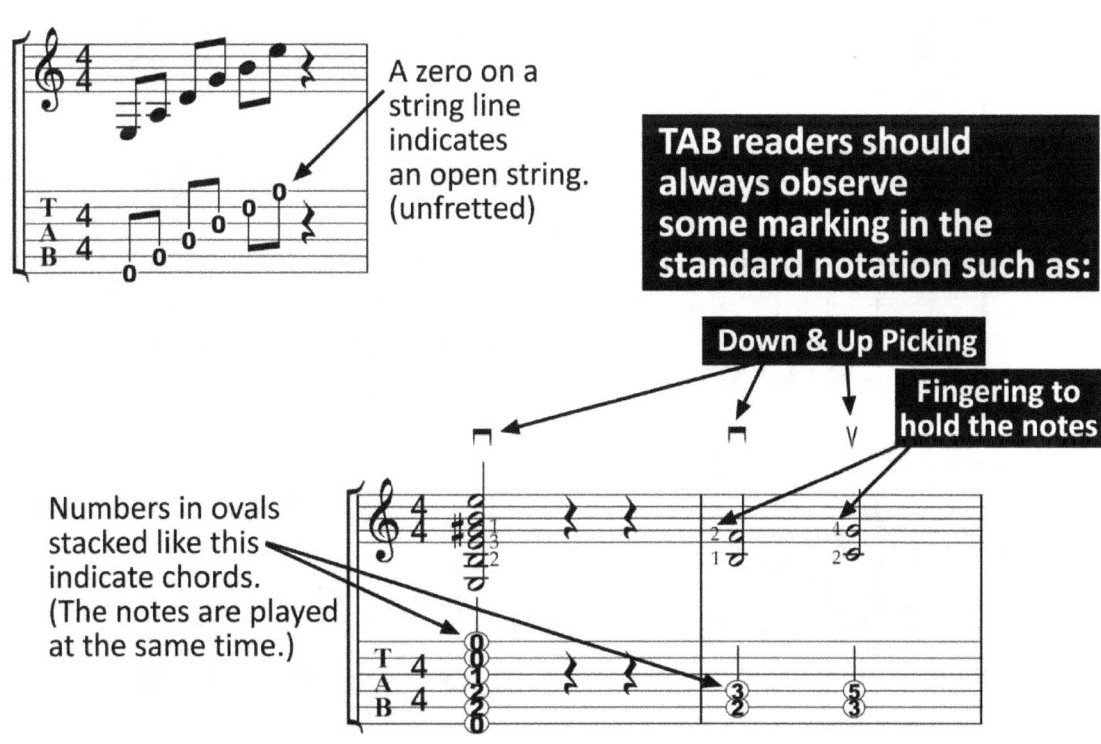

THE NAMES OF THE NOTES ON THE GUITAR

A few things to observe:

Some identical notes have 2 different names, a sharp name and a flat name.

Some identical notes are found in multiple locations on the guitar.

At fret 12 the sequence of notes repeats.

Below and on the facing page see the notes as they look in standard music notation.

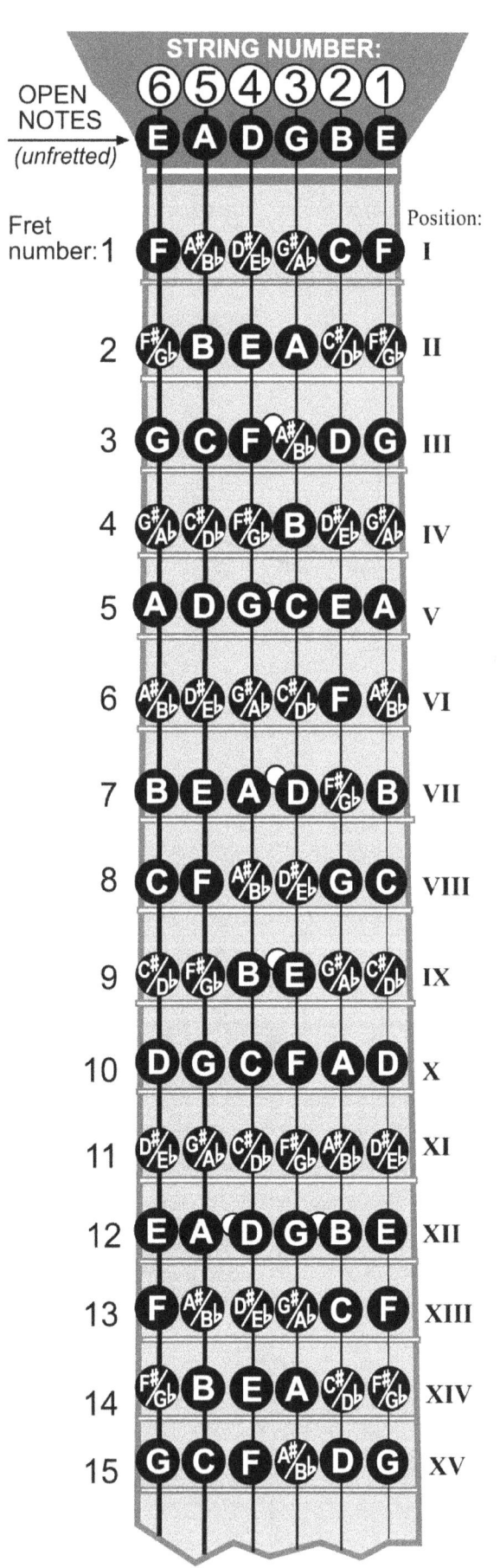

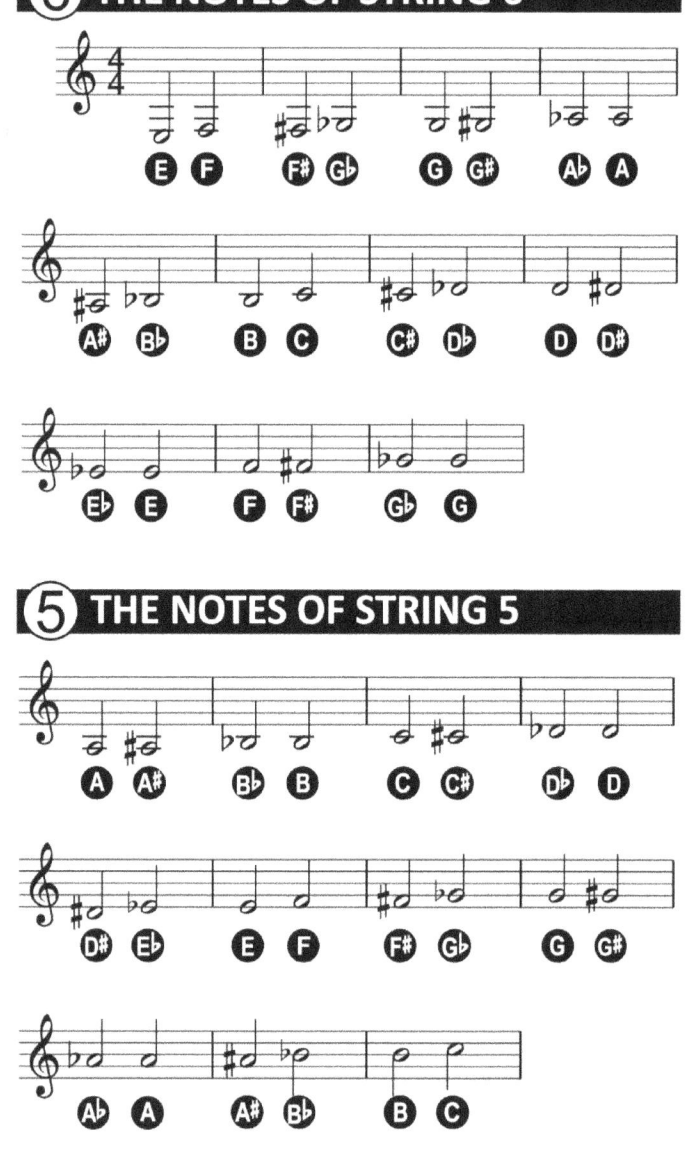

④ THE NOTES OF STRING 4

③ THE NOTES OF STRING 3

② THE NOTES OF STRING 2

① THE NOTES OF STRING 1

The information in this section will help beginners develop a firm physical foundation to facilitate playing the 20 Minute Excercises with optimum results.

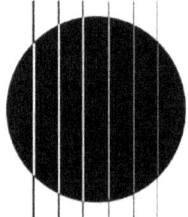

STRINGS
Sets of guitar strings vary in thickness, from very light to heavy. For optimum performance of these exercises a **medium weight** set of strings is recommended.

THE PICK
Guitar picks come in many shapes and thicknesses.
A **Heavy Standard Shaped Guitar Pick** is recommended.

Some manufacturers will mark the thickness with words others with numbers. Heavy would be .88mm - 1mm.

HOLDING THE PICK

Relax your RIGHT HAND at the wrist.

Place the pick **on the side** of your index finger at the top.
Extend the tip of the pick just below the tip of your index finger.

Wrap your thumb over the pick, perpendicular to the index finger.

Hold the pick between the **back of the thumb** and the **side of** the top of **the index finger**.

Don't use the tip of the thumb to hold the pick.
Don't flex the knuckle of the index finger backward or forward.

The pick should extend about this far beyond the tip of the index finger.

You don't need to grip the pick extremely tightly.

RELAX! Holding the pick with the back of the thumb against the side of the index finger gives the pick great stability for accuracy and maximum speed.

HOLDING THE GUITAR

The guitar neck should be at a good angle for optimum reach and maneuverability of the LEFT HAND. While playing, it is important NOT to hold or support the guitar with either hand.

When seated the guitar should rest on the LEFT LEG. Holding the guitar this way frees up both hands to play.

A foot rest under the left foot will help keep the guitar neck at a good angle.

When standing a good guitar strap should be adjusted to achieve a good angle with the guitar neck.

USING THE PICK

Pick and strum from here, not here.

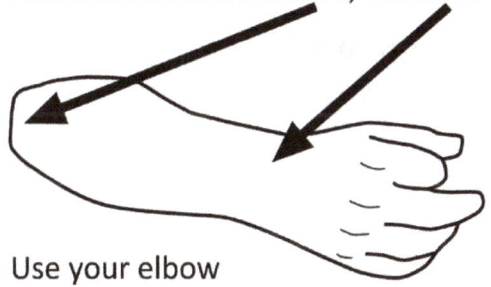

Use your elbow to move your forearm up and down as a solid unit.

Pick from the elbow, not the wrist.

Do not rest any part of the picking hand on the guitar.

Your pinky can slide along the guitar or pick guard. Fingers 2 & 3 can lightly touch the other strings without sounding them, **but allow the forearm to move freely.**

RELAX.
Avoid muscle tightness in your forearm.

**Chop...
as you would with an axe.**

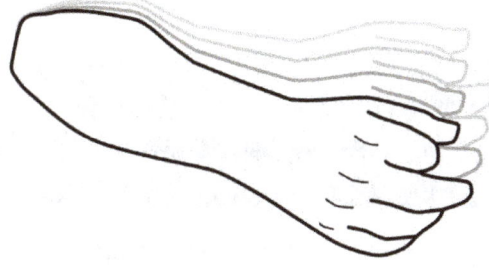

It is important to develop even and consistent up & down pick strokes & strumming.

Beginners should practice using all down strokes at first. Use the following REBOUNDING EXERCISE to develop consistent upstrokes.

REBOUNDING

The REBOUNDING EXERCISE helps the player develop strong & consistent down & up picking.

A string sounded without fingering a fret is called open.

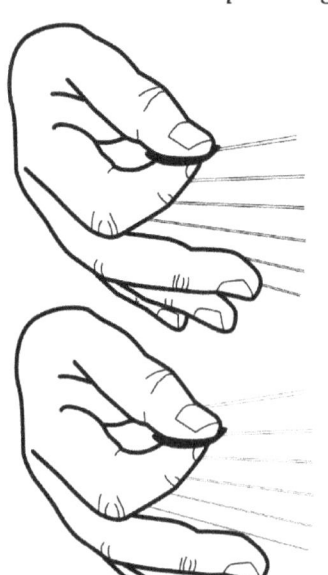

Using a downstroke play the open 6th String...

...lightly touching the 5th String below with the pick. *(Do not let this string sound.)*

"Rebound" back up, landing the pick just on top the 6th String.

Play the open 6th String 8 times using this rebounding technique.

Continue, play the open 5th String 8 times, rebounding off the 4th string:

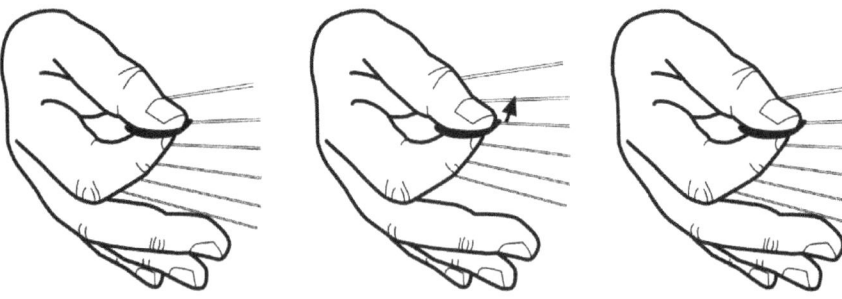

Finish the exercise by playing the the rest of the open strings 8 times each, using the rebounding technique described.

Obviously, when playing the 1st Open String, there is no string below to rebound from. When playing the 1st String the player should strive to make the upstroke match the spacing of the previous rebounded strings.

Never rebound using the string above, it is unnecessary.

HAND POSITION ON THE NECK

When fretting notes the thumb should be at the back of the neck.

This allows the hand to move easily up and down the neck and to comfortably stretch the fingers to achieve maximum reach.

Don't cluch the neck. A space should be here between the neck and your hand. (A pencil could fit in this space.)

Play on your fingertips as much as possible.

When performing large stretches, as in Exercise 9 (Stretch Exercise), the thumb is at a more exaggerated position at the back of the neck.

In these cases, placing the thumb closer to the front side of the back of the neck will afford the player maximum stretch and reach on Strings 4, 5 and 6.

HAND POSITION FOR A BARRE

Fretting more than one note at a time with a single finger is called a **barre**. Covering all six strings with the index finger is called a **full barre**.

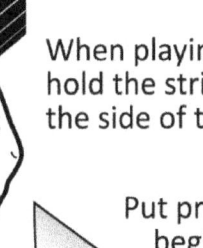

When playing a full barre hold the strings with the side of the index finger.

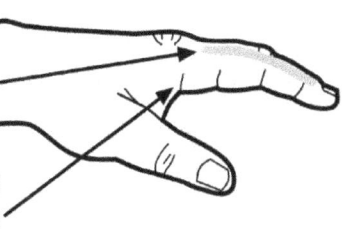

Put pressure on the strings beginning at the knuckle nearest your palm.

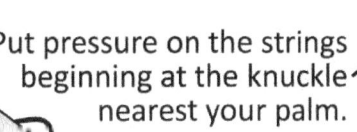

To hold a barre easily, especially a full barre, the thumb should be at the back of the neck.

www.ingramcontent.com/pod-product-compliance
Lightning Source LLC
Chambersburg PA
CBHW081259170426
43198CB00017B/2846